Ariel Allison

Daddy
Do You Love Me?

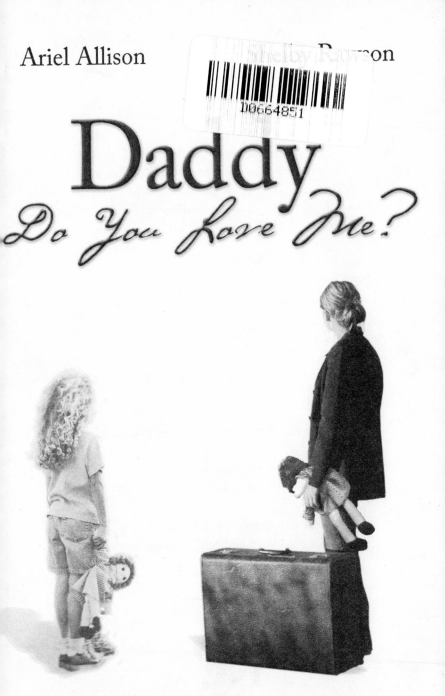

A Daughter's Journey of Faith and Restoration

First printing: July 2006

ISBN-13: 978-0-89221-658-1
ISBN-10: 0-89221-658-1
Library of Congress Number: 2006928495

Cover by Janell Robertson

All Scripture is from the New International Version of the Bible unless
otherwise noted.

Printed in the United States of America

For information regarding author interviews, please
contact the publicity department at (870) 438-5288.

Please visit our website for other great titles:
www.newleafpress.net

New Leaf Press
A Division of New Leaf Publishing Group

Dedication

Shelby would like to dedicate this book to the two most influential men in her life. "My Dad, for giving my wings the freedom to soar on this project. I love you. And my husband, Davy. You have never given up on learning the music to my song. That makes my heart sing more than you know."

Ariel would like to dedicate this book to her husband, Ashley: "Without you, I would have never found the strength to listen to my heart or to pursue my father. Because of your love, I have never felt afraid, ashamed, or abandoned. You are the best gift I have ever received."

Acknowledgments

How can we even attempt to say thank you to the people who have made this book a reality? Thank you just doesn't seem to cut it.

For Jonathan Clements, you are far more than an agent; you are a friend of the truest kind. Thank you for not only believing passionately in this book, but participating in the journey. Thank you for relentlessly trying to find a home for it, and not giving up, even when we did. Words cannot convey our appreciation. And to your wife, Missy, thank you for the nights and weekends you sacrificed your husband so he could work on this project. Your encouragement and your heart are priceless.

To Tim Dudley, Laura Welch, Jim Fletcher, Brent Spurlock, Amanda Price, and Judy Lewis at New Leaf Press, thank you for having faith in this project and making it happen. Thank you for listening to our hearts and letting us tell a story that so many need to hear.

Lloyd Shadrach, Robert Lewis, Dennis Rainey . . . thank you a thousand times over! Each of you have spoken words of truth that have changed our lives.

A thousand thanks to the brave women who have shared their stories in this book. You have been strong and courageous, and your tales of heartache and triumph will move the hearts of countless women. We love you.

To our husbands, your support and encouragement has been vital. We could not have done this without you. For London and Parker, thank you for being patient with Mommy while she plugged into the computer and did little but write for three months. For Kinsley, thank you for giving Mommy time on the "puter" to write and for your forgiveness when she lost her patience with you. Mommy always looks forward to your beautiful baby blues after a long writing session. For baby Oakley, thank you for waiting to make your entrance into this world until your mother could get the manuscript done!

To our fathers, we want to say that we are thankful for you, and thankful for all that you gave us. We have wrestled with you, longed for you, and loved you. Because of you we have shed many tears, but we have also laughed until we had bellyaches. While you may not realize it, you have pointed us home, to our true Father, and that is a gift indeed.

And to that Father whose fingerprints are all over this book, and throughout our hearts, thank You, Daddy, for taking two lonely, wounded women and redeeming our hearts. You are indeed the lover of our souls. This book is our offering to You, our way of trying to thank You for breathing new life into broken lives. We love You, Daddy, and we long to be held in Your arms.

Contents

Foreword

*L*et me introduce you to two courageous young women that I have grown to admire as I read their stories in the pages that follow. Ariel Allison and Shelby Rawson have written a story of remarkable candor and bravery which has birthed in both of them unexpected confidence and renewed trust.

What makes their book universally applicable to their generation is the common experience almost all 20- and 30-something women have had with their fathers. The breakdown of the family through divorce, affairs, workaholism, neglect, and other factors has yielded fruit in their children unanticipated by these parents. It's not that all fathers are failures. Some have been, to be sure, but all men are fallible in their role as dads. It is literally impossible for any one of them to do it perfectly, and so their inevitable imperfections and mistakes and oversights will leave their daughters feeling inadequate in small or very significant ways.

Do you wonder if you are loved? Did your father tell you he loved you? Did he demonstrate that love in positive, confidence-building ways?

If you question his love, if you feel inadequate or unsure of who you really are, I challenge you to follow the path in the pages ahead with Ariel and Shelby, who will soon become two new friends. Let them guide you into your own journey of faith and restoration. The road may be crooked and bumpy, but the end of every faith journey is always worth it.

Join them. Step out in faith and believe.

I promise you will be rewarded.

Barbara Rainey

Barbara Rainey is a frequent speaker at Family Life Conferences on marriage and parenting, along with her husband, Dennis, the executive director of FamilyLife. She has co-authored several best-selling books with him, including *Moments Together for Couples* and *Building Your Mate's Self-Esteem*. The Raineys have been on the staff of Campus Crusade for Christ for 27 years. They have six children and eight grandchildren.

Introduction

This is not a *self*-help book, and it was never intended to be. There are times in our lives when we discover a pain so deep that we cannot help ourselves, heal ourselves, or re-invent ourselves. Some of life's questions have no easy answers. There is no formula. There is no strategy. There is only a beginning, a starting point, a first step on a long journey that will change our lives.

Let us walk together. Let us lock step, lock arms, and lock hearts. We can survive the pitfalls and ruts, roadblocks and detours that lay before us, and perhaps even a wreck or two. After all, life is not a destination, but a journey, and some roads we were not meant to walk alone. This is one of them.

An invitation lies before us to heal — truly heal — and experience something we have never known . . . a Father who truly loves us. That may mean pulling back the scab on our hearts, and licking some old wounds. There will be fresh blood and fresh tears, but there will also be a stronger beat and a healthier pulse. It will not be easy, but it can be no more difficult than where we have been.

This book is not just for those women whose biological fathers pricked their hearts. We know that many of you reading this have had little or no influence by that father. However, there has more than likely been someone — whether stepfather, mom's boyfriend, grandpa, or adoptive father — who played the role of "Daddy" in your life. Whether you called him Bob, Daddy Tom, Grandpa, Dad, Father, or Papa . . . he should have loved you well. You were meant to be your daddy's little girl.

As you read the following pages, you are going to feel a lot: the good, the bad, and the ugly. You have our permission to throw this book at the wall, to write on its pages, and use it as a Kleenex if need be. Just remember as you read that we are with you, and we can relate to everything you are feeling. You are not alone.

We encourage you to jot and journal as you pour through these pages. Record the memories, chew on your thoughts, and ponder a new place of healing and restoration.

Journey to the Past

Heart, don't fail me now.
Courage, don't desert me, don't turn back
now that we're here.
People always say life is full of choices.
No one ever mentions fear
Or how the world can seem so long
Or how the world can seem so vast.
Courage, see me through.
Heart, I'm trusting you,
on this journey to the past.
Somewhere down this road, I know
someone's waiting.
Years of dreams just can't be wrong.
Oh, arms will open wide,
I'll be safe and wanted,
Finally home where I belong.
Well, starting here my life begins.
Starting now I'm learning fast.
Courage, see me through.
Heart, I'm trusting you,
on this journey to the past.

Aaliyah,
Anastasia motion picture soundtrack

Daddy's Little Girl

Chapter 1

There's two things I know for sure.
She was sent here from heaven
And she's daddy's little girl.
— Bob Carlisle
"Butterfly Kisses"

This is my journey, journey through life.
With every twist and turn,
I've laughed and cried as the road unwinds.
This is my journey, and I've learned to fight
To make me strong enough, to lift me up,
To bring my dreams alive.
In my desperation, I swore never again.
— 911
"The Journey"

I walk a lonely road,
The only one that I have ever known.

Don't know where it goes
But it's home to me and I walk alone.
— Green Day
"Boulevard of Broken Dreams"

*S*he wandered through the mall, just killing time. Her mind seemed to be blank, dulled from the TV-like white noise created by busy shoppers. So far she'd spent about an hour searching for the perfect outfit. She knew he loved simple, feminine things, and she wanted to see his face light up when he picked her up for their date. She'd just look in two more stores.

Why are all these clothes designed for a size two with no hips and an impossibly perfect posterior? I'm in decent shape . . . but to wear this stuff I should have started on a "Buns of Steel" routine when puberty hit — and never quit. Back pockets and zippers longer than two inches are my friends! Depressing. Time to move on.

There's a little ice cream shop. I could use a milk shake right about now. Hmm, what flavor? Banana is always a good choice. And it's a fruit!

Sipping on her milk shake, she spotted a little girl and her dad.

They must be having a daddy-daughter day together.

The father wiped his daughter's face as the ice cream dripped down her chin. He kissed her on the forehead, and offered a smile full of delight. Her entire little body seemed to beam as she grinned back at him.

All that just because of a kiss from her daddy.

She realized she was staring at them, unable to take her eyes away from the scene. She sat motionless as memories paralyzed her.

Snap out of it! You don't even know these people.

Too late. The tears ignored her desperate blinking and seemed to take her face hostage.

Not here. Not now. Please God. I'm over this.

But her heart drove her back. . . .

She was five with carefree blue eyes and a dimple made for a Welch's grape juice commercial. She was going to be a ballerina. And a nurse. Oh! And a fireman. She had saved many kittens and knew she was qualified! All of her dolls loved to hear her to sing, and her kitty, Socks, was never stuck in a tree for long.

It was Friday. Dad would be there soon. Her little heart anxiously anticipated his arrival. She couldn't wait to hear the car pull into the

Daddy, Do You Love Me?

driveway, the slam of the car door, and finally the sound of his key in the lock. Nothing could keep her away from the front door. After what seemed like days, she heard it. He was home. She made a beeline for him.

"Hi, Dad!" was greeted by a tired smile and bothered gaze.

She pressed on. *Surely he'll notice my special dress, or how I fixed my own hair. I know I look prettier today than yesterday. I've been good all day. My teacher said I was doing great in school. I cleaned my room. Maybe if I stay really quiet, that will please him. Maybe if. . . .*

"Gee, Dad, maybe if I'd never been born, that would have pleased you," she muttered as the milk shake froze her fingers. And she raced forward 25 years to the present.

Why couldn't he just say it? Or say anything? How hard can it be to tell your five year old that you love her? Or maybe a hug? Stroke my hair. Something. Anything. Anything but nothing. Nothing but questions and unrequited longings.

That was in the past. She was done with it. Life goes on. She was a big girl now. She didn't need a daddy anymore. She was all grown up, and she had a date tonight. When he opened the door, she *would* WOW him.

QUESTIONS OF THE HEART

Won't she? Can she? Can *you*?

Do you WOW him? Who is this guy? Your date? Your boyfriend? Your boss? Your best friend's husband? The guy at the bar? The guy on the bus? Is it your daddy?

Did he tell you he loved you? Were there strings attached? Did he hold you and tell you you're beautiful? Were there expectations that came with that hug? Did he tuck you in at night? Was he even there when you went to sleep? Did you wait for him to pick you up on the weekends? Did he come? Did he tell you he was proud of you? Did he play with you?

Maybe you have forced the questions so far to the back of your mind that the mere mention of them feels like swallowing shards of glass.

You are not alone. Let me say it again. YOU ARE NOT ALONE. Women have walked the road you are on. Women have crawled this road you are traveling. Maybe you feel like the road is walking on you and you're tied to feelings you've desperately tried to bury.

You are normal!! Yes, *normal*. The feelings you're experiencing from the past are not some freakish thing. They are the result of a wounded heart — a wounded heart that has never been healed. Stuffing your feelings and

Ariel Allison and Shelby Rawson

making yourself forget is a natural reaction. It's one of those lovely things called a defense mechanism. You did what you could to protect yourself and your fragile heart. For some of us this started as tiny little girls. Your young mind came up with ways to guard your bruised heart. It kept on making those guards as the years passed, trying so hard to keep it in one piece.

Your story may be different, or it may be very similar to the one you just read, but you and I have something in common. There is a piece of our hearts that is empty. It aches when we see a father walking through the park with his daughter on his shoulders. It shuts down when we hear another woman talk with love and admiration about her father. It bleeds in those moments that we are most honest with ourselves, when we admit that we really do want to be daddy's little girl. Sadly, the truth for far too many of us is that we never were.

I know an abundance of women whose stories are unique, but only in the details. The end result is always the same. They have lost their fathers. They have stories of intense pain, incredible longing, unabashed shame, crippling hurt, but most importantly, they have stories of hope. They know what it feels like to long for a father who isn't there. They know abandonment, abuse, neglect, indifference, ridicule, and unmet expectations. They know the secrets of *your* heart and they know why you have picked up this book. What they say to you today is that you are not alone.

THE LONGING

As much as we hate to admit it, we are in part who we are because of the man that gave us life. With the exception of your husband, if you have one, your father is the single most important man in your life. It can be frightening to know that he held the power to shape you into a confident woman who feels loved and admired, and that he also held the power to crush your spirit and leave you feeling as though you have no value in this life. The worst part is that we had no choice in the matter. We didn't give him that right, he has it based solely on the fact that we share his DNA.

The question for us is, do we even realize that he has shaped our idea of who we are? If so, are we able to accurately pinpoint the affect he has had on our lives?

In Norman Wright's, *Always Daddy's Little Girl*, he states the following:

Daddy, Do You Love Me?

Your father is still influencing your life today — probably more than you realize. For example, your present thoughts and feelings about yourself and your present relationships with other men reflect your father's impact on you. So often, what a father gives to his daughter affects her expectations toward the men in her life. Similarly, what a father withholds from his daughter can also affect her expectations toward other men. . . . If you were to describe your relationship with your father, what would you say? How has your relationship with your father affected your relationship with other men, your career, and your feelings about yourself? [1]

Sometimes, the hardest part is not accepting the truth about our lives, but living with a longing that may never be satisfied. The easier thing to do is stuff the ache somewhere deep down inside where we won't visit it again because, in essence, a longing is something that tugs at our heartstrings and makes us hunger. We ask ourselves, why we would long for that man in the first place? Isn't he the one that did all the damage? Why would I even want him to be part of my life?

But we do. We may not want or need the man that he really was, but we most certainly want and need the man he should have been. Admitting to ourselves that it is a good thing to want love from the man that gave us life is not a weakness, but a strength.

The longing is a good thing. A right thing. A hard thing. A painful thing.

DANCING WITH DADDY

Every little girl was made to dance, to twirl around in circles in front of her daddy and feel like she is the most beautiful girl in the whole, wide world. You read that and your heart went cold. You may want to close the book, or perhaps even throw it at the wall, because that dream didn't happen for you. You were never called princess. Maybe you were never daddy's little girl. I certainly wasn't. I can't even write those words without feeling somewhat of a twinge. I can't imagine what it would have been to feel like a princess, but I want to. I have longed for that my entire life.

The dream of dancing on your daddy's toes still plays in your mind. Only it's never your dad's face and you're never the little girl. You had no dress that he admired. His shoes never bore the weight of your stocking feet. Yet your dream refuses to die. Unwillingly, your heart breaks again

Ariel Allison and Shelby Rawson

as you beg your mind to put it to rest. You ask yourself why you must keep dreaming of the impossible.

Why am I torturing my wounded heart? Why can't these feelings just disappear?

Because you were meant to dance. You were meant to be lifted across the floor in a powerful caress. A sparkle is made for your eyes as love and adoration meet them. You cannot let go because your heart is stronger than your scars. The cries of your soul are louder than the weeping of your wounds. You are made for *dancing*.

Remember *Father of the Bride*? It's a great movie. Steve Martin plays this perfectly insane and amazingly doting father. He and his daughter had the whole sliding-down-the-banister memory, shooting hoops, and the chats. How can we forget the heartwarming talks they shared? It's just a movie. No biggie. So why was I jealous? It wasn't even real! I mean, come on, whose dad likes them *that* much? My dad certainly didn't. Shooting hoops usually involved at least one scolding when a jammed finger brought a few tears. I felt more like a disappointment than a daughter to be doted on. So why the jealousy? Why the ridiculous tears?

Because that's supposed to be me. I want my dad to get all silly and crazy over me. Me. Me!

Sometimes the longing goes unrecognized for what it is, a restless emptiness. I am surprised when I find myself shedding random tears at a song or when I watch a movie. In those moments, my heart leans forward, desperate to feel beautiful and safe and delighted in.

In Luther Vandross' song, "Dance With My Father," he speaks the longing of my heart, and gives words to an unfulfilled desire:

> Back when I was a child
> Before life removed all the innocence
> My father would lift me high
> And dance with my mother and me and then
> Spin me around till I fell asleep
> Then up the stairs he would carry me
> And I knew for sure I was loved.
> If I could get another chance
> Another walk, another dance with him
> I'd play a song that would never, ever end
> How I'd love, love, love to dance with my father again.[2]

Daddy, Do You Love Me?

How I'd love to dance with my father period. Not again, but just once, even a moment of uninterrupted adoration, just because he loved me, just because I'm special. I don't have any memories like that. So I must find my satisfaction, and admit my longing, in the song that illustrates what I was denied.

SO IT BEGINS

And so the journey begins. We know our current condition, broken and afraid. Our future destination feels vague and unsure, because we don't really know where we are going. We hope. We believe there is something better on the other side, but we don't know for sure. However, today we hover on the edge, waiting to leap, afraid to fall, and wondering if we will be caught. As with any journey, we must take the first step, perhaps into thin air, not knowing where we will land. So we set out on this journey with a confession; it means that we must acknowledge that we are broken. We are damaged goods.

Ariel's Thoughts

I was 25 years old the second time I went to a counselor to talk about my father. I was married, the mother of a little boy with another on the way, and I couldn't escape the whisper in my mind that said I was robbed of something. The scary thing was that I knew the whisper was right.

Jeff came into the office, greeted me, and took his place in a chair beside the desk. He leaned forward and asked the question I had heard him say several times before, "So why are you here today, Ariel?"

I hated that question because I often didn't know the answer. Sometimes I just hurt and didn't know why. That day was different however, I knew exactly why I'd come.

I hung my head and could barely choke out the words. "My father has been dead for three months and I don't miss him." It was the truth, but I felt evil for admitting it. No good daughter would say such a thing.

I *sobbed*, not because the vacuum caused by my father's death was unbearable, but because I didn't feel the ache at all. I tried to tell myself that if I felt anything at all, it was relief. It had been an incredibly difficult relationship. The things he did were inexcusable. That grave held more than a body; it held the crushed dreams of a little girl. He'd taken them with him when he died.

Ariel Allison and Shelby Rawson

Jeff leaned in, compassion etched on his face and said, "Has anyone ever told you, to your face, out loud, that you had a really *crummy* father? Has anyone ever told you that you should have been able to dance for him and know that he delighted in you? But he didn't. He *chose* to miss out on you, and the only hope you had of being daddy's little girl you buried in November."

I gasped, mouth open, and eyes large, partly because of the guts it took to spell it out in black and white, and partly because it was true. I shook my head.

"See," he said. "Now I know your secret. I know the one thing you have kept to yourself all these years."

I had known it all along. It *was* my secret, but my secret was out in the open now and it was agonizing. Someone else knew about the deepest wound of my soul. What I missed was not the physical presence of my father, it was what I had never gotten, what I would never get; the *love* of my father. Until the last breath faded from his body I had hoped that things would change, but that day I found myself sobbing because what I had hoped for my entire life was gone. I would *never* be daddy's little girl. Never.

Shelby's Thoughts

As I think about this ideal that we women have of being daddy's little girl, sometimes I don't know how I've felt. I've learned so many defense mechanisms to protect myself and avoid my feelings that there have been times when riding a turkey seemed a more likely occurrence. It took me a long time to admit to myself that I wanted and missed my dad's attention. Instead, I convinced myself that I wasn't striving to gain his notice, I was merely overachieving because I wanted to do it. Besides, we hardly spoke at all any more. Who could possibly need a relationship with someone who doesn't seem to want you anywhere near them?

Then I left home for college. Academically and socially, everything was going pretty fantastic. Grades were good, and friends were not in short supply. I had even decided to stay there for the summer to work and hang out.

Meanwhile, my parents were preparing to go to court and deliberate the allocation of my college expenses. (There had been some disagreement as to who was responsible for what portion.) Little did I know, a bombshell was about to explode in my heart. After a phone conversation with my

Daddy, Do You Love Me?

mom, I learned that I was expected to appear in court very soon. Not only did I need to go, but I would have to testify on my own behalf.

The day came. I became the picture of a nervous wreck. Crying was not enough to release the tension, hesitation, and fear that gripped me. (Thankfully, I was able to collect myself before taking the stand.) Mom's lawyer questioned me. No big deal. Then my dad's lawyer began. Forty minutes later I was excused. Even at this moment, a lump makes a bed in the pit of my stomach and my eyes well with tears as I recall those eternal 40 minutes. That man badgered me. Over and over he asked me the same questions about money, money, money. Mom's lawyer objected. Dad's lawyer persisted. I sat there while knots tied themselves through my body, and he did nothing. My dad didn't make a peep while his horrid lawyer beat me over the head with questions. Finally, the judge put an end to it. My seat could not have found my posterior any faster.

Then it was time for Dad to be examined. I think that hurt worse than the badgering. He was being questioned about my grades and activities in school. At that time, I was carrying an A average, had plenty of credit hours under my belt, was working part-time, and was active in many different clubs. (I never carried less than an A- average and always participated in numerous activities.) So when the lawyer said, "Shelby's always been a hard worker, hasn't she?" and my dad's reply came back "No, she hasn't," the crushing of my spirit and wounding of my heart screamed inside me.

That was when I started to realize just how much I was seeking some sort of affirmation from my dad, hoping that he would notice something neat about me. I think I lost hope that day. Hope soon became replaced with questions. The questions became so unbearable that I began wishing for it to end — all of it. After receiving my first letter from him during my second year in college, I became somewhat hysterical. No, not the screaming and ranting kind of hysterical. This was a dreadful, hopeless, sad, and hurt kind of thing. It was after midnight and the tears refused to rest, so I went for a drive. As I drove, I begged God to let another car cross the line and hit me. Or, maybe someone would run a red light or a stop sign. I finally pulled into a church parking lot. Thank God that a friend who cared about me found me that night. For this person, I am eternally grateful.

Yep, I was alive. The questions were, too. I wanted to know why I was never good enough. Why I was never pretty enough. Why I wasn't his

Ariel Allison and Shelby Rawson

favorite. What was it about me that he thought was so horrible? Daddy's little girl? Yeah, right. I felt more like daddy's little disappointment. Or if you'd prefer, you could have called me father's little failure. I was angry. I was hurt, and I was determined to be done with it. I wasn't going to seek his favor any more. If only life were so simple. . . .

Off in the distance, in the deep caverns of my heart, there was a tiny, tiny voice desperately wanting to be heard. My walls were hiding it. My defenses were choking it. *Shut up! Shut up! You don't know what you're asking. . . . You want the impossible. You still want to be daddy's little girl.*

Endnotes

1. Norman Wright, *Always Daddy's Little Girl: Understanding Your Father's Impact on Who You Are* (Ventura, CA: Regal Books, 1973), p. 10.

2. Luther Vandross and Richard Marx, "Dance With My Father," (J-Records, 2003).

Daddy, Do You Love Me?

Damaged Goods

There is one thing I must tell you. You must NEVER, NEVER let go of their hands. They will help guide you, but you must never let go. She asked their names, and the Lord said, Sorrow and Suffering.

— Hannah Hurnard
Hind's Feet on High Places[1]

Chapter 2

We are the broken
You are the healer
Jesus, Redeemer, mighty to save.
— Lynn Deshazo and Gary Sadler
"Be Unto Your Name"

When my father and mother forsake me, then the LORD will take care of me (Psalm 27:10; NKJV).

$\mathcal{D}$addy stopped hugging her when she was in the ninth grade, the year she began to develop breasts. The embraces from her father dwindled from tender hugs to the one-arm pats guys give one another when they are nervous about touching. The changes in her body were coming fast and furious, and the more womanly she became, the more uncomfortable he got.

She will never forget the day their relationship changed irrevocably. Her boyfriend had come over to meet her parents before taking her to Homecoming. Daddy called her into the office and sat her down sternly, "I don't want any pettin' going on. You hear?"

She had no idea what "pettin'" was, but her father wouldn't look her in the eyes and she felt dirty. He continued to withdraw from her during her high school years. Any rules regarding boys and dating were delivered through her mother, making her feel as though daddy was too embarrassed to talk about such things. The way he approached, or rather, didn't approach the subject made her feel guilty even though she'd done nothing wrong. Subjects like sex and body changes were taboo. She began to grow ashamed of her sexuality and her feelings toward the opposite sex.

It was during those years of insecurity about her body and emotions that she gave in to the attention of boys and compromised her values. She was hungry for physical affection, hungry for a sense of self-worth and beauty. Her choices were never discussed with her father. After all, he had taught her that such things weren't to be talked about.

In his attempt to create boundaries, he failed to teach his own daughter healthy boundaries. Instead of fighting his fears and personal struggles, he gave in to them. With no warning, he abandoned her. While he should have been equipping her to face the world, he put up his own guard and left his little girl to fend for herself. And so she did. . . . And so did we.

I'M NOT DAMAGED

Does the title of this chapter sound a little too drastic? Damaged Goods? Maybe this sounds more like the description of a prostitute? Perhaps you don't feel too damaged — a little bruised, but not broken. Or maybe this strikes an all too familiar chord that you manage to keep hidden behind one of your many walls.

Maybe no one has ever taken the time to tell you how fragile a little girl's heart is. That hope for a hug when deferred not only makes her tiny heart sick, it leaves a mark. That longing for love and praise should be met with reassurance — not rejection. That chasing of her dreams should be about being a teacher, a mommy, a dancer, a doctor — but it shouldn't mean chasing after her father's love. Shoot, this may not sound like you at all. You've always known your dad loves you. He just had a funny way of showing it. Right?

Me? Damaged?

So you don't have any self-image issues. No questions about your self-worth. You have wonderful self-esteem. You're never concerned about what a man thinks of you. I don't believe you! If you're reading this book, let's be honest. There are questions that tug at your heart and sometimes plague your mind. More than likely, there are times when you are teetering between an emotional breakdown and emotional paralysis, and those walls you keep up, they serve a very good purpose. Crutches usually do. Believe me, I know. They don't require a lot of maintenance these days because they've been there for a really long time. Maybe you've tried to venture outside your walls, or at least stuck your hand out to check the temperature. Smack! Yep, just in time to have it cracked by someone. Enough of that. You decided to stay where it's safe — a little cold, a little lonely — but safe.

Maybe this isn't even close to your story. Perhaps your life appeared just as perfect, or perfectly crazy. I don't know . . . but you do. I'll remind you again, there is a reason you are reading these words. Your heart begged you to do it. Now it's time to give your heart a voice. It is pleading for an audience. Will you listen? Will you have the courage to speak for your heart?

Life happens. Your story. Life with or without your dad. What happened? What did he do? What didn't he do?

You're mad. You're hurt. You're empty. You're clueless as to why you keep repeating the same behavior . . . why you can't have a deep relationship . . . why it is so important for men to notice you . . . why you react so strongly when you think you're left behind or rejected . . . why you can race in a downward spiral at the drop of your emotional hat . . . why you throw your body around casually like an old coat . . . why you must have a boyfriend at all times . . . why you can't say your father's name without cursing inside . . . why you keep your husband at arm's length.

DADS MATTER

You need to sneak a peek at your life and the choices you've made — whether consciously or unconsciously. In addition to that, you need to look at your family of origin. If you come from a broken home, you are at a much higher risk of making poor relational decisions yourself. According to *Divorce Magazine*:

> Fatherless homes account for 63% of youth suicides, 90% of homeless/runaway children, 85% of children with behavior problems, 71% of high school dropouts, 85% of youths in prison and well over 50% of teen mothers. The number of single-parent homes has skyrocketed, displacing many children in this country. Approximately 30% of U.S. families are now being headed by a single parent. In 80% of those families, the mother is the sole parent. The United States is the world's leader in fatherless families.[2]

A little sobering isn't it? We live in a culture that says dads don't matter. Everything we hear on television and much of what we hear on the radio says that men are powerless, impotent, and unimportant. It is the era of man-bashing, but those of us raised by single mothers know the truth. For that matter, those of us who had uninvolved fathers know the truth as well. Dads matter. They matter immensely!

Just how did your relationship with your father affect *you*? Are you walking around in a brick box? Your own little fortress forged from many years of guarding the castle housing your heart. Or is your heart bleeding uncontrollably on your sleeve? Willing and ready for anyone who is able to bind it up with a Band-Aid — when what you actually need is reconstructive surgery.

Are you the walking wounded? Do you understand what it is that needs to be healed? Do you even understand how it was that your father hurt you? You don't want to hurt any more. You don't want to be angry . . . to place blame . . . to cry when you look in the mirror and see the shape of his jaw and the color of his eyes.

For all I know, you don't want to shed another tear over a man who was ignorant to his failing for most of your life. So don't cry for him. Cry for yourself. Grieve a little. Grieve a lot. Now pick yourself up off the floor and survey the damage. Don't grovel in it. Look at it. Look at yourself. Don't rationalize your choices, behaviors, or responses. If you're like me, then you may be surrounded by red flags — so many that you're overwhelmed. Yikes! Breathe. This is a starting point, not a jumping off (a cliff) point. Put one foot in front of the other. Have a little conversation.

Daddy, Do You Love Me?

"Self."

"Yes?"

"We're damaged."

"Uh-huh. I know. It's about time you said it out loud!"

"Geesh. Go easy on me. I'm new at this."

"Okay. Let me start for you. Our esteem is really low. You try not to let anyone see it, but we're dying in here. And all the guys . . . well, they're not helping."

"Geese oh peesy. Got it! Enough already. I can only handle so much at once."

Deep down, you knew the crud was a-creeping. It has been laying in wait. You were running from it hoping it wouldn't pounce and knock you lower than you already feel. The thing about crud and mud, murk and mire is that it hates to be brought into the light. It's like nasty mud being hit by the sunshine. So shining a little light on the mire you're drowning in has a bit of a choking effect on it. It dries it up, causing it to crack and break into a million pieces. So it can be blown away. Yep, your cruddy choices and painful past may have left their mark, but you don't have to let them keep you down any longer. Keeping them hidden allows them to have more power than you know. Admit they are there, bring them into the light, and take away their power to control your life.

Don't believe the whispers in your head telling you that bringing up your uglies will only hurt. That is a big, fat lie. Freedom is behind the fear. Isn't that what you want? To be loosed from the millstone you've been lugging around your neck like a noose? Absolutely! Lighten your load, one lie, one whisper, one fear at a time. Embrace your struggle. Stand up in this storm and take it, take it full in the face.

LICKING OUR WOUNDS

This is going to hurt a little bit, maybe a lot. We are going to pull back the scab and inspect the wound. It's been festering down there, waiting to be cleaned out.

We are going to look at the damage. We are going to see it and recognize it for what it is — sin. We were wronged. We are going to grieve and we are going to take the capstones off our hearts.

A few brave women have shared their stories with us, the good, the bad, and the ugly. We are going to walk that dark road with them for a few moments and we are going to survey the damage. Sometimes it is a little easier to look at someone else's life and recognize what went wrong. It is much harder when it comes to our own. Things get complicated. We make excuses. We get confused. We rationalize. So instead of trying to inspect our own hearts right now, we are going to look at some obvious neglect in the lives of other women. Hopefully, that will enable us to begin recognizing our own issues. We are going to see their wounds, but we aren't going to stay there. The damage isn't the end of the story. There is always something more.

CARRIE'S STORY

The letter fell like a feather as my dad dropped it casually out of his hands and into the garbage can. A few moments earlier, I'd run outside to greet him, and as usual, he brushed me aside, in a hurry to get in the house. He was always in a hurry to get somewhere.

I'd been writing him love letters for about a month; you know, school girl crush kind of letters, telling him how handsome he was and how I wanted to marry someone like him when I grew up. Every day, after I finished my schoolwork, I would seal it with a prayer and a kiss, and then place it under his pillow. He never mentioned the letters. So that day, I decided I would ask him if he'd been receiving them.

After he got out of our new station wagon, he opened the back door to collect his briefcase and stethoscope. I grabbed his legs and told him I had a question. Without breaking stride, he made his way up the sidewalk, checked the mailbox and climbed the stairs.

"Daddy," I beckoned, "Daddy, please listen." I was standing still in the foyer, but he kept walking. I waited for him to turn around but he never did. All I saw was the back of his head as he browsed through junk mail. I was used to seeing the back of Daddy's head.

"Yes," he answered, seeming put out. "What is it?"

"Daddy, have you been finding my love letters under your pillow?" My feet shuffled and I turned my gaze downward. I could feel the shame turning my cheeks into beets.

As I watched him drop the unwanted junk mail in the basket with the rest of the trash, I wondered if that was where my heart-felt efforts ended up also.

"Yes, I've been finding them." Then he went to his room.

That was it. Ouch. It stung to be left standing there alone. Was this all he could give me after I'd poured out my heart?

Daddy, Do You Love Me?

During my middle school and teen years, I remember feeling so rejected by numerous episodes such as this that it was like a valve got turned off in my heart to protect it from further pain. I remember making conscious vows to stop feeling. I succeeded in becoming hard and bitter, but not having any hugs or words of affirmation from my dad left this girl desperate for affection, or even validation. At a very early age I ran into the arms of the first man who looked my way. I still feel plagued by feelings of insecurity that literally take my breath away.

Sadly, history often repeats itself in family patterns of relating. I see, in hindsight, that my dad was indeed giving me all he had to give, at least most of the time. Not having been loved well himself left him without resources. Not having the Holy Spirit or the revelations of God's Word left this brilliant, sought-after doctor ignorant and passive on matters of the heart.

As a young Christian, I had a hard time calling God "Father" — the only example I had of a father managed to acknowledge my existence with verbal and sexual abuse, was unfaithful to his wife, and did my homework just to keep me from asking questions. When confronted with the impact those actions had on his daughter, he said, "All men think this way. You've always had a tendency to overreact."

God has made His Name known to me in astounding ways as "Heavenly Loving Father." His healing touch has the power to override all the other information found in a human heart. Now that my wounded soul is able to call out "Abba Father," I know He has me well on the road to recovery. After walking with Jesus a while, I know that hope is a sure thing. Hope has a Name.

WHAT IS YOUR STORY?

If you are anything like me, you probably feel as though you have lived that very moment, even though the actual experience belongs to someone else. Perhaps your throat became dry, or you were blinking back tears. You probably wanted to take that man by the shoulders and shake him. How could he ignore his precious little girl? How could his heart not be moved by the love letters of a child? Then the thoughts begin to turn inward. You know how she feels because you have been there yourself, and it hurts. There was a time in your life that you so badly wanted your daddy. How did you go from that trusting little girl to the woman you are today? How did your heart become so damaged? Why does it hurt so badly to explore this area of your life?

Ariel Allison and Shelby Rawson

What is your story? Have you ever thought it through? Or have you pushed it so far to the back of your mind that bringing those memories forward will require revisiting wounds that you swore you would never think of again? Will you have the courage to admit that you cannot do this on your own?

Each story looks so very different. Each pain is unique. For Carrie, it was emotional abandonment and even sexual abuse.

Let's see what it looks like for two other women.

ROSEANNE'S STORY

I don't think the tragedy of my relationship with my dad is based upon what he did wrong so much as it revolves around what he didn't do at all. My pain has been caused by what was not said, what was not done, and a general lack of follow-through.

The breakdown in our relationship began the day he and my mother separated. I was three years old and I was standing in the driveway beside his truck while he was moving out. As he loaded his records into the floorboard, I wept and begged, "Please, please take me with you!"

It wasn't so much that I wanted to go as that I did not want him to leave. Even at that age, I knew what was going on, though neither he nor my mom said the words out loud. He said no and left. I can't ever remember feeling completely loved and accepted by him after that.

Have you seen the movie *Hope Floats* with Sandra Bullock? There is a scene in which the father leaves. It was very much like that. When I first saw the movie, I was weeping hysterically at the end of that scene. I hadn't realized until the scene change that I was out of control. I was in the theater wailing and howling. It was awful. I felt like I had just relived one of the most tragic days of my life.

I have always made excuses for Dad about how he didn't mean to hurt my feelings. I bottled up my wounds since he apparently meant no harm. It took me years to realize that I wasn't being oversensitive — I had been under-loved.

When I was five years old my dad got re-married and I was not invited. I felt replaced by a new family, and unwanted at such an important event. Now I know that the wedding was the day after his divorce from my mom was final. She would not have allowed me to attend even if he had invited me. Then Dad adopted his new wife's son, Chuck, because his father was not around. Over time, I wasn't jealous of the attention Chuck received,

Daddy, Do You Love Me?

but I became resentful of Dad's involvement in his life in comparison to no involvement in mine. It seemed hypocritical that everyone thought he was so great for being involved, but . . . what about me?

When I was in third grade, Dad moved to Florida to be in the Navy. There was no communication (except on my birthday, Christmas, and maybe Thanksgiving) and rare visitation. Our phone conversations were extremely minimal. I very specifically remember calling once and the first words out of his mouth were, "What do you want?" I was crushed.

My expectations for him were minimal, but more importantly, my expectations for men in general were minimal. I grew up thinking that my father was "super-dad" because that was all I ever knew. I had never been told that it should be different, not even by my mom.

I wrote my dad letters. As a little girl I would pour my heart out to him without any response. I chased after him, longing for a glimpse of unconditional acceptance. I don't remember consciously thinking that, but I wanted attention like only a father can give. Perhaps the only reason I recognize it now is because the pursuit of my father displayed the same dysfunction that I had when I began dating.

Dad has always told me that he loved me — repeatedly — and he has repeatedly apologized for not being the father he should be. Every time I see him he does this, even now. It seems honorable that he would apologize, but his first apology was when I was 14, at which time I was still clueless to his shortcomings. It seems that he could have taken advantage of my naivete and become the father that he wanted to be . . . but he did not. I confronted him about all of this when I was 21, 23, and 25. Each time, he said he was sorry and that he loved me, but there was no change to our relationship. I had heard those empty words for so long, so many times, that they fell on closed ears.

After living for a third of a century without a father, I do not know how to be a daughter. Even sadder, I do not have the desire to be a daughter.

I recently gave birth to a son. Some people say that having children softens your heart because you want your kids to know their grandparents. This is not true for me. I find myself wanting to protect my son from the disappointment that I have lived over and over. I know that my son will experience hurt, but I do not want it to be from someone that I tell him he can trust.

I do have one good thing to say. I hate to admit it because I stubbornly like to think that I only have bad things to say about my dad.

Ariel Allison and Shelby Rawson

My walk with the Lord has been greatly influenced by my father. I went to church with him while visiting him once in Florida. People were expressing their love for the Lord like I had never seen. They had joy and it was easy to see that their love of God was growing — not just a place to go, or thing to do on Sunday. There was a change in my heart during that time. Perhaps it was in my pursuit to have his approval, but whatever the reason, God used this man who has broken my heart over and over to bring me to himself — to bring me to the Healer and Lover of all.

SINKING HOPE

In a way her story sounds more like sinking hope than floating hope doesn't it?

Oh, yes. I've seen the movie *Hope Floats*. Or should I say I've cried in *Hope Floats*. I know exactly to which scene she is referring. It ties a knot in my stomach to recall the little girl following her dad to the car. He is trying to leave to be with his new wife and he has no plans to take his daughter along.

BERNICE: I'm coming with you, Daddy!

She runs upstairs and packs a bag, then races back down to his car. She throws her little suitcase in the trunk. He pulls it out. She tries again. He pulls it out. She tries to get in the car with him, pleading.

BERNICE: Daddy, what are you doing?

He locks the door. Tears stream down her face as she screams that she wants to go with him. Bernice is left crying out at the top of her lungs.

BERNICE: Daddy, don't leave me, I love you. You want me, I know you want me!

Her father appears disinterested through her wailing, seemingly oblivious to the emotional wreckage he's causing his daughter. He drives off in a cloud of dust, as she screams hysterically on the sidewalk. She has just been abandoned by her father. He has chosen a mistress over her. Not only did he cheat on her mother, he cheated on her.[3]

You betcha I cried in that scene. I cried for that poor, little girl with whom I could empathize. I cried for another little girl who wanted to take a front seat with her daddy — me.

What little girl doesn't want to be chosen by her father? How could such abandonment not wreak havoc on the tender heart of a little girl? We wonder how there can be redemption for little Bernice.

Daddy, Do You Love Me?

Yet one movie reviewer described it perfectly when she said:

> The story of *Hope Floats* doesn't end with Bernice weeping and abandoned. Birdee and Bernice get to see how hope rises from the ashes of their broken dreams and make a new dream. As Birdee's mama says, "That's why they invented families — so hopeless wouldn't have the last word."[4]

WENDY'S STORY

At about age 14, when all the emotions and stresses of being a teenager were in full force, I really began to feel the strain on my relationship with my father. Along with my first year of high school came first dates, first boyfriends, and the need for more independence from my parents. I think my father really didn't know how to handle these big changes. It was then that I noticed that he became more of a dictator than a father. We were never allowed a voice or an opinion about things. His attitude was one of, "My way or the highway," and I was often lectured for hours at a time.

My family had always attended church and my father was a very strong figure there, yet his images at church and at home were totally different.

I think it was around this time that I started to feel resentment toward church. My parents became active sponsors in my youth group and would accompany us on trips. My dad was so fun, patient, and compassionate to other kids; everyone thought I had the greatest dad. What they didn't see was that I was being compared to the other girls in the youth group. There were constant comments like "*Why can't you be like so and so,*" and he would always allude to other girls being so good and talented. I remember that I started to feel very uncomfortable, as though I didn't fit in and wasn't like everyone else. I started to see those girls that I was compared to as better than me.

High school brought many experiences that would change my life forever. When I was a sophomore I was raped by a friend's boyfriend. I never told my parents. I just knew that somehow my dad would blame me, and it would be more than I could handle. I suffered alone, and to this day they still don't know.

My junior year I transferred to another school and the partying began. Every weekend was an excuse to drink and smoke marijuana. Along with the partying came the really crazy relationships. Maybe it was my impaired judgment, maybe I just so desperately wanted someone to love and accept me. It caused me to use sex as a way to feel wanted, loved, pretty, and in control. I wasn't worried about my dad anymore. There wasn't anything I could do to impress him or get his approval so I just stopped trying. I'm sure he saw this stage in my life as total rebellion, when in reality I had completely given up on him.

By the time my senior year rolled around it didn't have to be a weekend to drink and smoke anymore. I'd skip classes regularly and yet somehow I still managed to graduate on the honor roll.

After graduation, my dad couldn't wait to send me off to college, but I was fine working at the mall and I decided to attend our local university. Besides, I had graduated to a new level of relationships, the abusive ones. My boyfriend would slam me against walls, push me through windows, and gouge me in the eyes. I was at an all-time low and I so desperately needed help. He had isolated me from my friends and I felt so alone.

I was 18 as I sat on the bathroom floor slicing my wrists with a razor blade. The pain was too much to bear. The hopelessness that I could never do enough for my dad to love me had led me to an incredibly dark place. I felt it must be my fault that I was in this terrible relationship.

I remember repeating to myself, *I just want to go home; I just want to go home.*

As I sat there in a pool of blood the thought of my mom finding me made me unbearably sad. I remember thinking that I wished she would just walk in so that maybe they would take me somewhere to get help. I just wanted to talk to someone, anyone. I cleaned myself up, bandaged my wrists and went to bed. A couple of days later my sister noticed the bandages and told my parents. I thought, *Finally, maybe they'll get me some counseling.* My mom cried, but what came out of my dad's mouth has stuck with me to this day. He sat me down, looked straight in my eyes and said, "Now that was a stupid thing to do, don't you think?" We never talked about it again and like so many other things, I just pushed it down and went on.

I continued on that self-destructive path for one more year and I found myself in places and situations I never would have dreamed I'd be in. It wasn't until my dad mentioned that I should attend our church's college study group that everything changed. Attending that study brought back so many of the feelings I had felt growing up. Once again I felt inadequate

Daddy, Do You Love Me?

and inferior. Coming from where I had been, it seemed as though I had nothing in common with them.

I soon met a group of people at the Bible study who had been in dark places like me, and recovered by the healing power of Jesus Christ. I met a dear friend who saw me in the hurt and pain that had haunted me for so many years. He prayed that one day God would heal my pain and restore my faith in Him. I opened my heart to Christ and began the very long road of healing. That dear man who prayed for me without ceasing, and saw something in me that I didn't see in myself, is now my precious husband. He has loved me unconditionally and helped me have a closer relationship with Jesus.

For years, I don't think I truly understood God's unconditional love for me. I couldn't grasp my Heavenly Father's love when I didn't even feel like my earthly father loved me. It wasn't until God blessed us through adoption with our beautiful son that I truly understood how much my Father in heaven loves me. He gave me something I could never have given myself in a time when I needed so desperately to know that He was there. To look at the precious face of that baby was, and still is, a daily reminder that God loves me. Unlike my earthly father, despite the things I've done to hurt and disappoint my Heavenly Father, He still loves me and always has. I am a wife, a mother, a sister, a daughter, and a friend. I am beautiful and worthy because my Heavenly Father tells me so.

UNLEASHING THE ANGER

Now let's be honest for a moment, shall we? I mean really honest, the kind of honest we aren't often allowed to be. It makes us angry to hear those stories. It is just so unfair. Abuse. Anger. Abandonment. Neglect. Why? Why on God's green earth does it have to happen?

I know you're angry at your father, but there is someone who you may be more angry with. God. Go on. Admit it. He let it happen and He could have stopped it. He could have given you a different father. He could have changed your circumstances.

Isn't it a little scary to go there, to admit that God ultimately has the culpability for your pain? It is pretty unnerving to know that the One you should run to with your broken heart is the One that let it happen? Pause just a moment as you let that sink in. It was *God* that allowed your pain.

You aren't going to hear that very often in church or in a Bible study. That kind of honesty doesn't come along every day, does it? God is not afraid of your pain, and He is not afraid to take ownership for the fact that He placed you in your circumstances. Don't mistake me by hearing that God inflicted your pain. That is not what I'm saying at all. I'm just saying He didn't stop it. Perhaps you wonder if that makes Him just as bad as your father, a willing participant.

So we come back to the age-old struggle, that thorny question that has plagued mankind forever: If God is loving, why does He allow bad things to happen to us?

Or to be more precise, *If God really loves me, why didn't He give me a different dad?*

> [Christians] face the fact that living in a fallen world sometimes exposes people to experiences that no bearer of God's image was ever meant to endure and that our reactions to those experiences are deeply stained with our own fallenness.[5]
>
> — Dr. Larry Crabb
> Foreword to *The Wounded Heart*
> by Dan Allender

If you are expecting a profound answer to the question of *Why*, you are gravely mistaken, but I will be profoundly honest. I've listened to all the arguments, I've read the theologians, and in my own life I am just now beginning to come to grips with the reasons for my own pain. And yes, I've got a lot of it — an absent father, stolen innocence, and bad choices. You name it. I've been there and I've walked that road. But you know what? There is one thing that we often miss in our eagerness to know *why*. We miss the opportunity to pursue God in our brokenness, our pain, and our raw anger. Let me reassure you. God is not afraid of us. We don't scare Him. The depths of our need and our desperation don't turn Him away or leave Him helpless. He knows what to say and He knows what to do. He knows *why*. He has the answer to your question. Why did this have to happen to me? *Why?*

> There are many options available to the Christian for dealing with past abuse, but the outcome is unappealing: forgive and forget — denial; pressured love — passionless conformity; quick cures — irresponsible passivity. It is not difficult to understand why the Christian who has been abused often chooses either to seek help outside the church or to learn to handle the damage

Daddy, Do You Love Me?

by pretending it does not exist. I strongly believe the Scriptures offer better ways of hope and change. What is the better path? The argument of this book is that *the best path is through the valley of the shadow of death.* The crags of doubt and the valleys of despair offer a proving ground of God that no other terrain can provide. God does show himself faithful; but the geography is often desert-dry and mountainous-demanding. To the point that the path seems too dangerous to face the journey ahead. . . . The journey involves bringing our wounded heart before God, a heart that is full of rage, overwhelmed with doubt, bloodied but unbroken, rebellious, stained, and lonely.[6]

— Dr. Dan Allender
The Wounded Heart

The question then becomes, do you have the courage to ask Him? I mean really ask Him, with all your hurt, and all your heart?

Perhaps you've gone there many times. I know I have. Yet as I think back to the prayers and conversations I had with God about my pain they seemed very banal for a long time, very polite. Something like this, "Dear God. My dad did a lot of stuff wrong and it really hurt and I don't like him for it, but I know that everything will work out okay in the end. I know that You are good and You are in control. Help me forgive him. Help me love him. Help me."

There is absolutely nothing wrong with that prayer. Technically, it is right. Theologically, it is sound, but it is heartless and it is devoid of the pain that I really felt. As I wandered farther down this path, and as I took a few more blows from my father, my prayers changed quite a bit. They weren't nearly so polite, but they were far more honest. I was given permission to be irreverent. I was given permission to really hurt.

As I think on the tears and the snot that I shed later on, I am reminded of a few scenes from the movie *Forest Gump*.[7]

Lieutenant Dan has lost both legs below the knees during a battle in Vietnam. Instead of leaving him on the battlefield to bleed to death, Forrest throws him over his shoulder and carries his friend to safety. Lt. Dan is furious at the world and he is furious at God. He is miserable with the circumstances of his life. He has become an alcoholic and he has turned to prostitutes to try and fill the searing hole in his heart. He is desperate and he is cramming his life full of whatever will numb the pain:

Ariel Allison and Shelby Rawson

LT. DAN: Now, you listen to me. We all have a destiny. Nothing just happens, it's all part of a plan. I should have died out there with my men! But now, I'm nothing but a [dog-gone] cripple! A legless freak. Look! Look! Look at me! Do you see that? Do you know what it's like not to be able to use your legs?

FORREST: Well . . . yes, sir, I do.

(Remember that Forrest had braces on his legs during most of his childhood. He is well acquainted with brokenness.)

LT. DAN: Did you hear what I said? You cheated me. I had a destiny. I was supposed to die in the field! With honor! That was my destiny! And you cheated me out of it! You understand what I'm saying, Gump? This wasn't supposed to happen. Not to me. I had a destiny. I was Lieutenant Dan Tyler.

At first we are shocked with his irreverence, but we also know there is a lot of truth in Lt. Dan's statement. This wasn't supposed to happen to us. Not to us. We had a destiny. We had dreams. We were princesses. We were queens. Then one of life's explosions happened in our lives and we lost something. We are crippled. We are broken. We are angry — angry at God.

Even so, the story continues. Let's go back to Lt. Dan. Let's see him face up to his pain and face up to his God.

LT. DAN: Have you found Jesus yet, Gump?

FORREST: I didn't know I was supposed to be looking for Him, sir.

LT. DAN: That's all these cripples, down at the V.A., that's all they ever talk about.

LT. DAN: Jesus this and Jesus that. Have I found Jesus? They even had a priest come and talk to me. He said God is listening, but I have to help myself. Now, if I accept Jesus into my heart, I'll get to walk beside Him in the kingdom of heaven. . . . Did you hear what I said? *Walk* beside Him in the kingdom of heaven. Well, kiss my crippled [rear]. God is listening? What a crock of [stink]!

As he screams these words at Forrest, Lt. Dan is pinned helplessly to his wheelchair, throwing empty liquor bottles across the room. It is a

Daddy, Do You Love Me?

sobering sight. He is crippled and we know he will never walk again. It seems as though he has been given empty promises.

Scary and honest. And you know what? Appropriate. Don't tell me you haven't thought it, too. Do you think that just because you may not have said it out loud that God hasn't heard you? Let's be real. He knows when you're angry with Him and He can take it. Confessing your anger to God will not shock Him. He will not turn away from you blushing, and neither will He strike you with lightning.

The story doesn't stop with pain and brokenness and a crippled man stuck in his misery cursing God. It doesn't end there and our stories don't either. Let's go forward a few years in his life. Let's see what happens next. Lt. Dan is still festering in his anger. He has joined Forrest on a shrimping boat and together they are trying to make ends meet. It isn't working. Instead of shrimp, they are catching old shoes, tires, and garbage. After weeks and weeks of failure, Lt. Dan is at his wits end.

LT. DAN: Where the [heck]'s this God of yours?

The wind begins to blow strong.

FORREST: It's funny Lieutenant Dan said that, 'cause right then, God showed up.

Lt. Dan challenges God. He has been trying to make it work on his own the entire time. In his own strength he has been trying to find fulfillment and "get over" his wound. It isn't working and he can't do it anymore.

Water sprays on deck during a hurricane. Lt. Dan is on the rigging, shouting and shaking his fist as wind and rain pelt him.

LT. DAN: You'll never sink this boat!
FORREST: Now me, I was scared. But Lieutenant Dan, he was *mad*.
LT. DAN: Come on! You call this a storm. . . . Blow, you son-of-a-[gun]! Blow! It's time for a showdown! You and me. I'm right here. Come and get me! You'll never sink this boat!

TURNING THE CORNER

I am not advising my readers to become foul-mouthed sailors, but I am saying that it is absolutely appropriate to stand up in the storm, or crawl on all fours if you can't stand, and face the God who made you. Face the God who placed you in your circumstances, and pour it all out. It won't be pretty. It won't be polite. There may be rage and anger. There may be tears and sobbing. But how much better is it to pour it out on the One who can handle it, than the innocent ones in our lives? In that moment, in the deepest storm, in the moment of honesty and truth and desperation is when the God of heaven steps forward and greets His daughter.

There are times in our lives when our hearts should be reverent and quiet toward God, and times when we should be silent. There are other times when the gale force winds of sorrow push our hearts past the breaking point. In those moments, we can approach God with everything we've got.

Lt. Dan survives the storm, hurricane Carmen to be precise, and the next morning as a calm sky rises over that bay he has found something precious. There is nothing to fear in approaching the God of heaven and earth and laying the responsibility at His feet, nothing wrong in letting it go.

> LT. DAN: Forrest, I never thanked you for saving my life.
> FORREST: He never actually said so, but I think he made his peace with God.

Did you catch that? He thanked Forrest for the very thing that at one point he hated him for — saving his life. In effect, he was thanking God that his life hadn't turned out the way he thought it should. Lt. Dan believed that his destiny was that of every other member of his family, death on a battlefield, a casualty of war, but that is not what God had planned for him. That may have been the legacy of his father and his grandfather and his great grandfather, but God had something much better for Lt. Dan Tyler.

Toward the end of the movie, we catch a glimpse of Lt. Dan as an entirely different man. He is sober. He is married. He has gotten prosthetic legs and he is walking. *Walking!* It is not such a far stretch to think of him walking in the kingdom of heaven with Jesus now, is it? Lt. Dan has picked up the shattered pieces of his life. He has reclaimed his dignity and his worth. He has become a new man. He will always have the scars from his battle, he can't change that, but Lt. Dan has been given new life — a future and a hope.

What happened between him and God during that moment in the storm changed his life. It changed his life for the better.

Daddy, Do You Love Me?

Can you and I do the same thing? Can we do it in our brokenness? Can we do it with our admission that we are truly damaged goods? Emotional cripples. Walking wounded.

Defy defeat by your damaged goods. After all, they are your *goods*. Allow them to be mended. Take them back. Take your *goodness* back. That is who you are meant to be. "He who began a good work in you will carry it on to completion" (Phil. 1:6; NIV).

We saw it in Lt. Dan's story, and we saw it in the stories of the women we just read about. It doesn't end with defeat, brokenness, and gaping wounds on the battlefield of life. There is so much more to our stories, perhaps unwritten at the moment, but there is so much more!

FOR MY GOOD AND HIS GLORY

There is One who has walked a much more broken road than any of us. Yet, in His beatings He wept for us. He bled so our damaged goods could be redeemed. I am not worthy of His sandals, yet He would give me both if I asked. His balm is true healing. His heart is the essence of an eternal embrace. He knows my murky waters and He meets me in the midst of them. He is redeeming love. He is my Father. He is the one who knows my pain. He saw me in those moments when I hurt the most. He saw it, and He wasn't standing idly by watching. He wasn't defenseless. He wasn't complicit. He was holding my heart. He was calling my name. He *allowed* it for my good and for His glory.

So how in the name of Cletus do I grow past this, you wonder? How do I get to the point where I really know all of this was for my good and His glory? Hmmm. . . . That's a good question. You probably can't do it alone. If you can, you're *way* stronger than me. I needed a little help, a little motivation outside myself. I needed a little bit of God. Okay. I needed a lot of God. I needed to understand that there is a man who would never let me down . . . never leave me, nor forsake me.

You need to know what you are worth, what you deserve . . . how you deserve to be loved by a man — not just any man — your daddy. You need to know that you are a precious, priceless little girl, one who deserves to be told how pretty you are in your dress up clothes, what a great job you did jumping over the creek, what a beautiful song you sang, and how much Daddy loves you — just because. Grieve for this little girl. Grieve for yourself. Learn what life can look like with a loving Father. Believe it — not just in your head, but in your heart. Learn about love.

Ariel Allison and Shelby Rawson

THE DAMAGE WE CREATE

So where did your heart run? Did it run into the arms of the first man who gave you an opportunity to feel desired? Did it take the opposite direction and find security in performance? Those are the two extremes, we either prostitute our heart or we confiscate it. We either become Mary Magdalene or we become a Pharisee.

Somewhere between the first blow we took and the position we find ourselves in today, we crossed an invisible line. We *chose*, and it is such a delicate balance because it wasn't our fault. No five-year-old-girl deserves to be ignored, beaten, or raped. God knows we deserved something better.

So why is it that all these years later you have chosen a life that was formerly imposed on you? Why are you critical and judgmental of others when you cringed at the harsh words yourself? Why do you abuse your body with drugs and alcohol when the bruises left by raging fists marked your heart forever? Why do you scream at your children in anger when you cried uncontrollably at the torrent of words that were thrown at you? Why, for God's sake, do you sell your body to the highest bidder while the memories of your own molestation make you sick to your stomach?

Your life and your future is not the sum total of your experiences. John Eldridge says in *Wild at Heart*:

> I am astounded what young women will offer when they are famished for the love and affirmation they have never had from their fathers. They will throw themselves at a man to get a taste of being wanted, desired.[8]

It is an uncomfortable thing indeed to acknowledge that the wounds inflicted on us by another are intimately associated with our own sin. The sins forced upon us lead us into sin. We cannot escape that fact. We were hurt, therefore we hurt ourselves, others, and most importantly, God. The fact is that we make those choices on our own. We have much ownership in the circumstances of our lives. I am not talking about our abuse, but the choices we make because of that abuse.

> No victim is responsible for having been abused. But abuse does provide strong reasons, potent stories, to ask, "Where was God? Does He love me? Can I trust Him? If I can, what am I to trust Him for?" The devilishness of abuse is that it does Satan's work of deceiving children about God's true nature and encouraging them

to mistrust Him. Fearing to trust God, the abuse victim will naturally choose other gods to provide her with life, whether alcohol, promiscuity, or approval-seeking. The abuse victim's fundamental enemy, then, is sin: the fearful refusal to trust a God about whom she is deceived. The Spirit of God is hard at work in her to reveal God's true nature and confront her fear and mistrust, but His work is a battle that requires her cooperation[9] (Dan Allender).

Ariel's Thoughts

I hadn't combed my hair in days, and my little five-year-old hands were grubby. It was the middle of July and I spent most days by myself, running barefoot through the sagebrush. In some ways my life was magical. I lived in the country, at the foothills of the Rocky Mountains, and I had miles of National Forest and open mesa at my disposal. I could be anything I wanted to be on those lazy summer days. Sometimes I would be Lucy, from *The Lion, the Witch, and the Wardrobe*. Other days I would be Bilbo Baggins in search of adventure. I knew the stories by heart and lived them out during my playtime. It would not occur to me for nearly 20 years that my existence had actually been a lonely one. My only friends were characters in a book.

That day was different. I was making music. Earlier that week someone had given me an old guitar. It only had three strings, none of which were in tune, and it was so scratched and banged up that it would never make beautiful music again, but I didn't care. I sat on the toolbox of my father's old Ford truck and plucked at the strings for two hours. In a soft, hesitant voice I wrote a song — my first and only. I was so proud of it! Giddy with excitement I ran inside to sing it to my parents. The words didn't rhyme, there was no tune, and there was very little power in my voice, but it was my creation, my masterpiece! I plucked randomly at the loose guitar strings and sang to them.

No applause. No smiles. No hugs. No kisses. No nothing. I waited expectantly, hopefully, my heart beating fast.

"Well?" I finally asked. "What did you think?"

The answer was quick and certain.

"Ari, you can't sing."

Although my mother mouthed the words, the absolute silence from my father was just as devastating.

Ariel Allison and Shelby Rawson

Tears welled up in my brown eyes and I blinked them back. I gently set the guitar down and returned to my imaginary world outside. I never even tried to sing again. It had been uttered, in no uncertain terms, that that was something I could not do.

Brick number one.

I was eight years old and I begged and pleaded to go to work with my father. He'd been delivering pizzas at night for some time and often took my older brother along. They would spend the evening together, eating pizza, and waiting for an order to come in. Inevitably my brother would come home with a treat bought by Dad, a candy bar, a pack of gum, a new toy. So I asked him if I could go with him that night.

"No. I don't want you with me."

I ran outside and cried. I was surprised at the force with which my tears came. I hadn't made it past the door step, and lay where I had fallen, a sobbing mass of tears and snot.

He didn't want me.

A short time later my mother stumbled upon me, literally I'm afraid, and asked what was wrong.

"I don't understand, Mommy. He doesn't want to be with me. He always takes Samuel but he doesn't want me!" My little heart was shattered in a hundred pieces.

Mother was angry so she gave Dad a brutal verbal lashing. By the time I found the courage to go back inside, my dad shuffled his feet and said with no small amount of irritation. "I *guess* you can go." There was still no mention of him wanting me.

So I went, but only because I knew he would buy me candy. It's an odd thing to barter your heart for a little chocolate. The big Easter bunny brought the only sweetness of the evening. There was no conversation. I can't remember if he said a word to me all night.

From that day forward, every time my father got in the car to go with the family somewhere, I got out, slammed the door, and ran back in the house. I didn't want to go anywhere with him. I didn't want to be near him. On the rare occasions that we all had to go somewhere together, I sat as far away from him as possible.

Brick number two.

By the time I was 13 years old I can distinctly remember never being called pretty. Freckly. Tall. Skinny. But not pretty. I may as well have been Olive Oil from *Popeye*. My dad never once gave me a compliment

Daddy, Do You Love Me?

about my physical appearance — a comparison or two maybe, but never a compliment.

Lost in books or television, my father didn't comment when I dressed up or pranced in front of him. My twirling games of ballet were met with irritation and a swat as he requested that I stay out of his way. I never sat in his lap or got an affectionate hug.

"Go away, Ari, I'm trying to read the Bible."

Oh, yeah. You read that correctly. Shooed away so he could brush up on his end-times debate. Don't think I didn't have reason to hate God, to hate the Bible, to hate religion.

It certainly didn't help that puberty hit me like a ton of bricks. Over the course of one summer I went from gangly little girl to Jail-Bait. The body may change fast, but the heart and mind of a child takes more time.

Johnny was 18 and I couldn't believe it when he told me I was pretty. I thought my heart would explode. I wanted to hear more. I wanted to drink it in. I wanted to be hugged. I wanted someone to hold my hand and make me feel beautiful.

He wanted so much more.

The loss of innocence occurred so slowly that I didn't realize what was happening. I was afraid that if I told him to stop touching me or stop talking like that he would leave and I would be back in the same place where no one liked me and no one thought I was pretty. So I said nothing until the day that he demanded everything from me. I was only 14 and I was too scared. So I turned him away and he left for good, just like I'd known he would. If I wasn't willing to give him everything, then he wanted nothing at all.

I realized that day that I could use my body to get, and keep, the attention of men. I also realized that no one loved me, not this boy, and certainly not my father.

By now the bricks were too numerous to count, not a wall, but a fortress impenetrable. The only difference is that that my father was no longer building the wall, I was doing it myself.

Shelby's Thoughts

My parents had been divorced as long as I could remember. At first, going to school brought out a shyness and insecurity that often immobilized me. Every day I dreaded walking up to those double doors. I knew they were going to tease me. So far, it hadn't happened, but I believed

Ariel Allison and Shelby Rawson

it was just a matter of time. Thankfully, I discovered how much I liked school — and it seemed to like me back. Good grades came easily. Gym class was even fun. Pretty soon, I made new friends. We did all that silly stuff like comparing our book bags and flowered panties when the boys weren't around. (Oh, come on, you know you did that, too!)

At the end of the day I went home and waited for my sister to get home. We didn't get along too well. I was pretty certain that my sister hated me. I couldn't wait for five o'clock to roll around — Mom would be home.

Except for Fridays. Those days were spent in anticipation because my dad was coming. My sister and I got to spend every other weekend with him. He was so much fun. We would goof around having spit-wad fights and doing flips on the couch cushions, and most of the time, we went to my favorite place — Grandma and Grandpa's.

For the most part, it was really fun. It just didn't go too well if we got in trouble at Dad's house. A painful thump right between the eyes for not coming home when he called me was enough to burn itself in my memory for years to come. I can still picture his face and hear the tone in his voice before the sudden blow from his middle finger.

First and second grade were fun. I loved my teachers and continued to excel academically. Friday afternoons were still anticipated, but not with quite as much enthusiasm. My stepmother wasn't exactly warm and welcoming to my sister and me. The word "backseat" started to take on a different meaning for me shortly after my father re-married.

Oblivious to the stirrings inside myself, I had no idea my young heart was aching more and more to feel important. To be seen. To be heard. To be special.

Writing started to become a secret outlet for me sometime around fourth grade. This is the first thing I wrote in my Hello Kitty notebook expressing my emotions:

> We can't change what's already done
> We come in about fifth and they're number one.
> I don't like to run races that I can only lose
> You've seemingly decided that you must choose.
> You've made your choice
> It's perfectly clear.
> They're chosen first by you
> But our number isn't even near.

Daddy, Do You Love Me?

Soon bricks became my companions, building themselves up one by one around my innocence.

As I grew older, my desire to perform became more apparent and my need to make good grades a must. Being on the stage was increasingly appealing — even though it made my insides churn to the point of sickness at times. Nerves and a lack of self-confidence didn't help matters.

I put on a good face for those around me and for the reflection in the mirror. No one had a clue — including me — that my self-esteem was gradually getting lower and lower.

Friday afternoons were welcomed once more in the absence of a second wife. As was my usual routine, I would wait by the door at the same time, eager for him to come. Bags packed. I was ready for a weekend with my dad.

Some days, I would watch the clock as the minutes passed by only to hear the dreaded sound. R-r-ring! R-r-r-ring! Should I answer the phone?

He's not coming.

Hurry up. Go to your room. Get out your dolls and play. Keep playing. It's no big deal. Don't cry. Stop crying. He'll be here tomorrow. So what if he has to drop you off early? So what if it seems like he would rather be with your sister? It's okay. You're gonna be okay.

I stayed at the top of my class all the way through school. I participated in every activity I could squeeze into my schedule. Dating wasn't an issue. Enough guys asked me out. On the outside, everything looked great. So great, in fact, that people actually thought my life was like an episode of *Leave It to Beaver*.

My best friends were rock solid — just like bricks. Little did I know, I had made them my closest friends and enemies. I kept the real people in my life at arm's length for the most part. (It's a bit of a challenge to get genuinely connected to a pile of bricks.) Somewhere along the way I learned to make judgments of others rather quickly. That way, when they decided I wasn't worthwhile, I already had a reason for them not to be my friends. Whew. That tactical move seemed to make things much less painful for me.

And my dad? Well, we weren't talking too much those days. I was totally fine with it. Really. Except for a small meltdown here and there, you wouldn't have had a clue that we hardly spoke.

So, I headed off to college. My freshman year was stellar, with excellent grades and extracurricular activities out the yahoo. I was doing fabulous.

Ariel Allison and Shelly Rawson

(I did say *was*.) Then it happened. Out of nowhere, I was pummeled by an emotional grenade that hit with the force of a semi. Crack! It sent me reeling. What the —? What in the —? I was trying to figure out just what it was that blindsided me. Something was happening. Ouch. Ouch! Pain. No, not pain. PAIN. HURT. ANGER? And questions. No answers. Lots of questions.

I began unpacking the baggage of my relationship with my father and it felt horrible. For the first time, I began to taste some of the effects my life had had on me, and I couldn't spit it out. It clung to my tongue like burning coffee. It was a feeling that would become very familiar over the next several years.

Perfectionist. Yep, that's me. Performance oriented. Yep, that's me. Judgmental and self-critical. Right again. Why? Why were these things so ingrained in me? Because a kindergartner never stopped crying out for Daddy's attention and approval. The five year old would not let it go. . . . Could not let the question lie. . . . Daddy, do you love me?

Even amidst the ugliness and loneliness I'd grown to embrace, that pure and simple question begged an answer. Daddy, do you love me? I was standing up to my eyeballs in it, drowning in my damaged goods, waiting for an answer.

Endnotes

1. Hannah Hurnard, *Hind's Feet in High Places* (Carol Stream, IL: Living Books, 1975).

2. http://www.divorcemagazine.com/statistics/statsUS.shtml

3. *Hope Floats* (Twentieth Century Fox Film Corporation, 1998).

4. http://childofdivorce-childofgod.blogspot.com/

5. Dan Allender, *The Wounded Heart: Hope for Adult Victims of Childhood Sexual Abuse* (Colorado Springs, CO: NAVPress, 1990), taken from the foreword by Larry Crabb, p. 7–8.

6. Ibid.

7. *Forrest Gump* (Paramount Pictures, 1994).

8. John Eldridge, *Wild At Heart: Discovering the Secret of a Man's Soul* (Nashville, TN: Thomas Nelson, 2001), p. 146–147.

9. Allender, *The Wounded Heart: Hope for Adult Victims of Childhood Sexual Abuse*, p. 26.

Daddy, Do You Love Me?

The Dirty Words

Someone ran away with her innocence
A memory she can't get out of her head.
I can only imagine what she's feeling
When she's praying,
Kneeling at the edge of her bed.
      — Big & Rich
        "Holy Water"

in·no·cence: the state of being free from sin or moral wrong; lacking knowledge of evil.

I'm all out of faith, this is how I feel
I'm cold and I am shamed lying naked on the floor.
      — Natalie Imbruglia
        "Torn"

The innocent and the beautiful have no enemy but time.
      — William Butler Yeats

$\mathcal{S}$he was looking for her daddy's paint brush but found his magazines instead. She was deep in the process of making a picture for her father when she remembered the paint brushes that he kept in a drawer in the garage.

There were five magazines in all, the top one open to the page he had last been reading. Well, perhaps he hadn't been reading it, because there were no words.

The only other woman she had ever seen naked was her mother, but that was different somehow. That was *Mom*. This picture made her cheeks turn red. She stood on the stool for a moment, not knowing what to do. It didn't feel right to look at Daddy's pictures, but she couldn't turn away either. She quickly glanced back at the garage door, closed it tightly, and lifted the magazine out.

It took her less than ten minutes to flip through the pages, but what she saw would be forever burned on her brain. In later years, she would remember distinctly that the woman in the photograph wore bright red lipstick and nothing else. When she would think of what a naked woman should look like, that image always came to mind. Yet something else happened in her heart that day from which it would be much harder to recover. She began to believe that this was the kind of woman that Daddy thought was beautiful. *This* is what she should wear, or rather, what she shouldn't wear. This became her perception of what a woman should be.

Before sneaking back in the house, she made sure to return the magazine, open to where she found it. When she went back inside, she tried to finish the painting she'd started for her daddy, but it was an entirely different picture that filled her mind.

That day she didn't look at any of the other magazines, but over the coming months and years she viewed them all. Completely unbeknownst to her father, he had created and fed a growing addiction to pornography in his own daughter.

THE LOSS OF INNOCENCE

I close my eyes and I shake my head as I think about it, a little girl trying to please her father with a drawing finds his secret stash of pornography and her idea of sexuality is forever altered. It happens every day, countless times. It happens by accident, by careless fathers indulging their own desires at the expense of their children. And, *poof!* — her innocence is corrupted, just like that.

Daddy, Do You Love Me?

Maybe she's 5, maybe she's 15, it doesn't matter. What matters is that she now knows two things about her dad; she knows that he has eyes for women other than her mother, and she knows what men find desirable sexually. If she doesn't actually imitate it, she will beat herself up for not looking like the women on those glossy pages. She doesn't realize that the allure and beauty of those women is an unrealistic perversion of the glory that God intended her to have. No one tells her that. She is left to assume that a beautiful provocative woman is one who sheds her clothes for the world to see, and every little girl wants to be a beautiful woman one day.

As is the case with every lie, it is most effective when mixed with just a little truth. Pornography is so dangerous because it is three parts lie and one part truth. A naked woman is alluring and captivating and arousing. As well she should be. In fact, she is glorious and stunning. She was created in the image of God, and remember, she was originally created *naked*.

I love what John Eldridge has to say about this in *Wild at Heart*:

> Adam bears the likeness of God in his fierce, wild, and passionate heart. And yet, there is one more finishing touch. There is Eve. Creation comes to its high point, its climax with her. She is God's finishing touch. And all Adam can say is, "Wow." Eve embodies the beauty and the mystery and the tender vulnerability of God. As the poet William Blake said, "The naked woman's body is a portion of eternity too great for the eye of man."[1]

Porn doesn't just stop with pictures of naked women. It grows in its perversity until it bears no resemblance to that of Eve, walking naked and unashamed in the Garden of Eden. Even in its least offensive forms, it sets an impossible standard for women to live up to. Comparison kills.

ANGEL IN THE CENTERFOLD

It's embarrassing — disgusting, even. The images can be recalled in a split second. Why are they still there? Bl-u-u-u-ck! You never meant to see those stupid pictures in the first place. You sure as heck didn't know that you'd be stuck with them for the next umpteen years, either. It is not your fault that your dad had those horrible magazines. Here you are 20, 30, 40 years later . . . and the pictures are still vivid — the nasty, degrading shots of women — some of which had men, too.

You were just a little girl. At the time, curiosity kept you turning the pages. You'd never seen anything like this. It was weird, yet somehow provocative. *What on earth were they doing? Am I supposed to do that? Should I look like that? Is this the kind of woman my daddy likes? He must think these women are really pretty. I want to be pretty, too.* Your subconscious begins working overtime.

After some perusal, you close the magazine and put it back. After all, your dolls are waiting patiently! Days pass, perhaps weeks, and you haven't thought about those pictures at all . . . until one day when you're playing with your cousin. The two of you decide to strip down. (You're a big girl now. Six years old is perfectly mature.) You both just think it's silly. Harmless play, right? So why do you still remember it and feel gross?

You are newly married. You are bound and determined to be sexy for your husband. Mentally, you pick out your lingerie. Then, you put it on. Hmmm. . . . *This isn't having the same effect on me that I imagined. I don't feel sexy. I feel a little stupid. What if he thinks I'm not sexy? He'll probably think this lacey crap was a dumb idea.* Your internal battle has begun. The facets of your imagination are fighting amongst each other.

You can be sexy.

Are you nuts?

He will love this!

No. He won't. He'll reject you and think you're ridiculous.

Besides, you don't look a thing like you're supposed to. You don't look one bit like a seductive woman. There isn't any resemblance whatsoever to those women in the magazines. The magazines. Aha!! They've struck again. Somewhere in the back of your mind, you believe that you are supposed to look like the "angel in the centerfold." Or, at least, feel like you can for your hubby.

Has it ever occurred to you that those magazines or those movies had more of an impact on you that you imagined? I'll bet they have. Yuck. Why didn't your dad hide those dumb things better? Better yet, why did he have them at all? It sure could have saved you from some of the mental images that remain burned in your mind. In retrospect, it probably could have saved you from more than just some sordid recollections.

I can watch my own daughter and witness just how powerful a daddy's affirmation of her physical beauty can be. She has not reached two years old and already craves his acknowledgment of her appearance. If I've heard it once, I've heard it a hundred times, "Show Daddy?" Of course, I get a smile when I tell her she looks pretty, but it's not like the one for her daddy. That one is different. She doesn't know it yet, but it is.

Daddy, Do You Love Me?

If something clicked in the back of your five-year-old brain when you saw those pictures, it's pretty normal. It's only natural that your mind made a connection to what you perceived as your daddy's picture of beauty. For some of us, this impression was deeper than it was for others. You may have obsessed over your reflection your whole life. Nothing ever seemed quite right. You've probably never been able to pinpoint the reason you weren't satisfied with the girl in the mirror. Looking at yourself and longing to be someone else is like second nature to you. Curse those flippin' magazines! That was no angel in the centerfold. The devil himself pricked you with his little pitchfork the day you saw those repulsive pictures.

I'm not saying that body image issues are caused solely by girlie magazines. That would be completely shortsighted and naïve. Most of us haven't helped matters by picking up the latest issue of *Glamour* at some point in our lives. That tends to be the more obvious placing of blame. What I am getting at is the subconscious of a little girl that was rocked by the viewing of her father's pornography. Yup, there it is again. That dirty, embarrassing word — pornography.

You shouldn't have seen it. You weren't supposed to see it. A child's eyes were not meant to see, nor her mind to absorb the twisted presentation of something meant for splendor. There is splendor in a woman. There is loveliness in her being. If your beauty feels as though it has been soiled, you cannot remove the cerebral stain. However, you can cleanse yourself of this dark spot. Picturing those images probably makes you feel dirtier than the pages they were printed on.

In Dr. Earl R. Henslin's book *You Are Your Father's Daughter*, he states:

> A little girl learns very early on what kind of woman draws her father's eyes. . . . All too many daughters have looked in the garage for a tool or in their father's desk for a pencil and accidentally discovered his stash of pornography. The daughter looks at the photographs and naturally concludes that this is the kind of woman her father really desires, the kind of woman men want her to be. This wound in the daughter's soul may never be acknowledged, but it will impact her life on a daily basis. Her feelings of inadequacy in trying to live up to the image she sees may lead to a lifetime of struggle with her appearance and weight. This will not only impact her relationships with men,

including the man she may marry, but will also affect her ability to instill a sense of personal value and a healthy body image to her own daughter.[2]

THE ASSAULT ON WOMANHOOD

Few and far between are the girls who do not get sexualized at a young age. The statistics are scary. One in three women are molested by the time they are 18. Of the women who escape that horrible fate, the overwhelming majority will see pornography, watch movies with gratuitous sex scenes, or be forced to endure the perversion of "sex education" classes in school. Whether in the classroom, the locker room, or the bedroom, we are robbed of our innocence before most of us can wear a training bra.

We are naïve to think that the abuse we suffer as women is just fate, or an accident, or just part of life. No, it is intentional and purposeful. Our greatest Enemy seeks to destroy the hearts of women and leave us forever in bondage. John Eldridge elaborates on this in *Wild at Heart*:

> If masculinity has come under assault, femininity has been brutalized. Eve is the crown of creation, remember? She embodies the exquisite beauty and the exotic mystery of God in a way that nothing else in all creation even comes close to. And so she is the special target of the Evil One; he turns his most vicious malice against her. If he can destroy her or keep her captive, he can ruin the story.[3]

This destruction is especially effective in the area of sexual abuse. It works like nothing else to corrode her trust in men and her trust in God. Many young girls build upon those experiences by becoming sexually active, while a lesser few indulge in a fantasy world of pornographic addiction and masturbation. One in a million escapes perfectly unscathed.

In a recent church service I attended, the speaker asked how many of those present were told about sex from their parents, in a biblical context. There were at least one thousand people present, and three raised their hands. I did not. My education began early — on the playground.

Ultimately, this is such a sad reality because we are sexual creatures. We were made to have sex and sex is a *wonderful* thing. God created it and it is a beautiful picture of a Holy God when women delight themselves in the arms of their husbands, but the vast majority of women do not learn how to be lovers in the marriage bed, they learn it in the backseat of a car.

Daddy, Do You Love Me?

Most of us have sung along to John Cougar Mellencamp's classic, *Jack and Diane*. I know I have. Yet there is something incredibly sad and almost sinister hidden beneath that great beat and raspy voice. There is the echo of reality as to the loss of innocence that so many women endure.

> Little ditty about Jack and Diane
> Two American kids growin' up in the heartland
> Jacky's gonna be a football star
> Diane debutante backseat of Jacky's car
> Suckin' on chili dogs outside the Tastee Freeze
> Diane's sittin' on Jacky's lap
> He's got his hand between her knees
> Jacky say Hey Diane lets run off
> Behind a shady tree
> Dribble off those Bobby Brooks
> Let me do what I please.
> And Jacky Say
> Oh yeah life goes on
> Long after the thrill of livin' is gone.[4]
> > — John Cougar Mellencamp
> > "Jack and Diane"

Long after the thrill of living is gone, we are left trying to put together the pieces of our shattered innocence. Sometimes it's a boyfriend. Sometimes it is a family friend. Sometimes it is a family member. Although many women part with their virginity willingly, there are those that live with the memory that it was not their choice. *Not at all.* It was torn from them, perhaps one piece at a time, or in many cases, all at once. I would be doing a great disservice to many of my readers if I did not address the fact that an untold number of women suffer the horrors of rape. Some of those women suffer it at the hands of their father.

THE DIRTY WORDS

Rape. Incest. Molestation. No three words in the English language can create more fear in a woman's heart. No three words are uglier. No three words are more horrifying when used to describe a woman's experience with her own father. *How* do you recover from that?

There can be no darker place in a woman's heart than when she endures sexual abuse from her father. There is no more deadly place for a daughter's heart to reside than in the cruel bondage of a father's perverted embrace. It does not get any worse. It cannot get any worse than that.

Before going any further in this chapter, it is important to note that I do not have the time or room necessary to comment on the ins and outs of incest and other forms of sexual abuse. What I offer here is a fly-by view of that damage, and must admit that most of the wisdom I have gleaned, and will quote going forward is from Dr. Dan Allender, author of *The Wounded Heart: Hope for Adult Victims of Childhood Sexual Abuse*. He is considered, by and large, to be the leading expert on that subject, and I cannot stress how important I feel it is for victims of sexual abuse to get and read a copy of his book. That being said, I will move on and attempt to do justice to this devastating subject.

It is one of the great shames of our world that incest is a reality for some women. They have been taken advantage of and abused by the man who should have protected their innocence more zealously than any other, their father. Such a tender subject can only be addressed well by a woman who has endured and recovered from such horror. In this chapter we will hear from author Ann Cameron and see how she overcame fear of her father, found healing for her body and her heart, and was able to offer forgiveness to the man who stole so much. Ann is currently in the process of writing her story in the upcoming book, *Until Someone Hears My Voice: Hope and Healing for Victims of Sexual Abuse*. She has given permission to tell it here, with the prayer that it will provide an anchor of hope to women who have suffered this horror.

I DON'T CALL HIM DADDY
The story of Ann Cameron

I've got no problem with Jesus or the Holy Spirit. My issues are with the Father. That word evokes so much in me, so much that is difficult to explain. . . .

To look at me you would think I have the childhood memories of a typical little girl; playing in Mommy's makeup, twirling my skirts for Daddy, and dreaming about being a princess. After all, I look like a normal person. I laugh a lot. I am happily married with two beautiful little girls. As a matter of fact, my life looks almost perfect from the outside. I should have those memories, but I don't. I know nothing of innocence, nothing of childhood dreams. To look at me, you would never know that I am intimately acquainted with a dark and brooding pain that has changed

Daddy, Do You Love Me?

my life forever. The first time my father raped me I was four years old, and he continued to do so for the next ten years. The memories of my abuse assault me at the most unexpected times . . . when making love to my husband, when changing the sheets on my bed, when taking a shower.

At the risk of going too far, and pushing too hard, let me say something to women who have been in that hell, and let me say something to those trying to pull her out. There is no physical pain on this earth like a rape. The tearing, bruising, battering agony is something you don't forget. It can be a battle to embrace the tender touch of a husband and not relive the horror in your mind. The mere sight of blood can take you back to a mental torture chamber. The mind becomes a playground in which our worst nightmares relive themselves over and over. The reclaiming of our minds and our memories is just as real a battle as the reclaiming of our dignity and our ability to trust men. People assume that rape is a sexual crime. It isn't, it is a violent crime. It is about control and domination. It is about fear.

There are no words to describe what was done to me for ten years. And it wasn't just me. It was both of my sisters as well. My older sister Dana's memories are sketchy and few, but my younger sister Leigh remembers everything — every single detail. She never forgot, and those memories drove her into a serious battle with alcohol. The more I have conversed with my sisters, and the more our memories match up, detail to detail, the more I understand what I lost. My entire childhood, my innocence, my virginity, was stolen from me in the most brutal way possible, and not by a stranger. My own father stripped me of my dignity.

Victims of sexual abuse can suffer outcomes such as promiscuous lifestyles, substance abuse, homosexuality, insanity, suicide, or even a physical ailment. Often they experience a combination of the above. My older sister Dana ran to other men to find solace, and my younger sister Leigh drowned her pain with alcohol. Although the most rare, I endured the latter of those outcomes when I lost my voice for four years. My father told me not to say a word about my abuse. So I didn't. Not for four years. Not to anyone.

I spent four years locked in silence, and was forced to learn sign language in order to communicate. The ridicule I endured during my high school years was unbearable. Unable to speak, I was labeled a retard and freak. For some insane reason, my peers assumed that because I could not speak, I could not hear either, and they spared no mercy in their jesting and accusations. My journey to recovery took me to several states and over 25 doctors before discovering the physical deformity that nearly ruined my vocal cords.

As a grown woman, I look back at the first 17 years of my life and I feel totally robbed. So much was taken from me. How can a father rape his four-year-old daughter, and continue to do so for the next ten years? Why did no one come to my rescue? I could have been rescued, you see, because my mother knew about it the entire time, and she did *nothing*. She never said a word about it. She simply left me in the hands of a pedophile to be repeatedly brutalized.

I learned early on that fighting back left me with nothing but bruises. My consequences for not performing usually included a severe beating. On the rare occasion that he chose not to give me a sound thrashing, he would totally ignore me for days and weeks at a time, not even offering a single glance or word in my direction. His message to me was loud and clear, "You are worth nothing to me except physical gratification."

The physical impact of that abuse on my body has created one of the greatest sorrows of my life. Children are physically not meant to handle the rigors of sex, especially a rape, and certainly not for years on end. Due to the repeated abuse, a bone growth was formed that would later prevent me from giving birth vaginally. I did not realize this had occurred until I had to have an emergency C-section with my first daughter. I hate that my children have to be cut from my womb because of the sins of my father. I hate that I cannot experience the joys of a normal woman giving birth because of what happened to me.

It seems as though my loss has touched each and every area of my life and left indelible marks. Relationally, I have suffered through two divorces, and am now mercifully married to a wonderful man. Emotionally, I have been stripped and have only recently learned how to truly love and be loved in return. Physically, I lost my voice for four years, and suffered unspeakable damage to my body. Spiritually, I floundered, angry and bitter until I found Christ several years ago. As I look at the shattered pieces of my life, I find that the healing started when I allowed the God of heaven into my life. I am a masterpiece in progress, but even today I can't make sense of many of the brush strokes. So I hang in this balance between brokenness and complete restoration and I trust that there is great purpose to my life and even greater purpose to my pain.

I am learning that my life has worth, something that I did not believe for many years. I am learning that I am a daughter of the King, valued

Daddy, Do You Love Me?

and precious in His sight, but that belief is by faith most of the time. The word "father" is very hard for me, and I have often viewed my Heavenly Father through the lens of my earthly father. I am learning.

Joe has lost the right to be called Daddy, hero, and friend. Even more than that, he has lost the right to have a relationship with three remarkable women. There hasn't been, and barring a miracle will never be, restoration with my earthly father. He is evil and totally unrepentant. Not for a moment is he sorry for what he did to me, and I know that given the chance he would just as soon repeat it with my daughters. That relationship has been buried, both for my protection and that of my children. I know that likely there will be no happy ending in that regard, this side of heaven. Yet I *do* know that I have a Father. When I hurt the most with memories of Joe, I turn to Him to teach me what a father should be.

I was recently asked by a friend what forgiveness has looked like for me, and I find it very difficult to answer. For me, it is an ongoing process. I release each pain as it surfaces, and I return to the truth that I know. The only times that I think of Joe are when the insecurities and fears that haunt my life return. It is in those moments that I choose to forgive. I must remind myself that I do not live in that place anymore, either physically or emotionally. During my childhood I was trapped in a house with no locks, yet no way of escape. I am not trapped anymore and I will not live as though I am. I won't let him keep me in bondage any longer.

As I think of my relationship with Christ, and all He has done for me, I am reminded that forgiveness is the only thing that cannot be stolen. It has to be given freely, and so I choose to do so. I choose to give better than I got.

I still walk this road, sometimes with a heavy burden, but I am moving forward. As I look back at my journey, I wonder how my life could come so full circle. How did I go from being the broken child to a woman that others come to for help? Much to my surprise, my life has become a beacon to other women, and sometimes men. As of this writing, I have spoken with and encouraged well over 50 other victims of rape and incest, and pointed them in the direction of the healer. My message to them is that there is hope, and there is healing, and there is victory. But it cannot be found in a bottle or a bed. Hope is found in the person of Jesus Christ. Mercy is found in Him, and believe me, it is enough.

My journey to freedom is still an ongoing process, and likely one that I will continue to travel the rest of my life. To those women who are floundering in that emotional swamp, I would recommend that you get help. Do not walk this road by yourself. The authors of this book have provided a list of reputable counseling resources. Find a counselor and begin the process. Friends, hear me clearly on this, if you hear nothing else, *it is not the end*. There is no place on this earth that the love and redemption of God cannot reach, including the darkness of that pit. Believe me, I know.

RAPE OF THE SOUL

It is an absolutely horrifying thought. My skin creeps. My mouth gapes open. My gut wrenches. Words are stuck in my throat as I ponder my reaction to molestation or rape. Rage. Rage wells up in me when I think of anyone daring to violate and rob my sweet daughter of her dignity, childhood, and innocence. What kind of person would touch a little girl? You've thought it, too. What kind of sick, twisted man takes out his sexual aggression on an innocent child? My word . . . I would want to ridicule, unabashedly shame, and soundly batter any man who did this to one of my sweet, innocent loved ones.

Some freaky man puts his hands on tender youth and spoils it. At least, that's how most of us think of it, right? We imagine it as an outsider of some sort. Yet, in the back of our minds, we know. We don't want to think about it, but we know . . . the freak may be your father. Not your babysitter. Not a neighbor or sneaky relative. Your daddy did it. Your daddy is the one who came into your room. Your room, your safe place! He told you that this is what special little girls do. They touch their daddies and their daddies touch them. Maybe he never said a word. He just snuggled up against you in your bed. You, your stuffed animals, and your dad, in bed. His hands became your greatest fear, most heinous loathing, and perhaps, your most shameful longing. This was the only time he ever expressed affection. The hands that were meant to hold you in your sadness, pick you up in your pain and brush away a tear . . . those very hands left you without protection or safety. They weren't something you could run into. They were something from which you fled.

Your dad should have been meeting your needs. Instead, he met his own. He should have been making sacrifices for you. Instead, he sacrificed your virtue. He stole your self-worth. He corrupted your purity. In their place, you were left with undue guilt and unjust shame.

Uuughhh. I don't want this to be your story. I don't want this to be the pain that you've experienced. Yet I know this may only scratch the

Daddy, Do You Love Me?

surface of a wound that is etched in your soul like the color of your skin. You cannot change it. You are unable to escape it. It's just there. Waiting for you in the darkness of your room. Waiting for you behind closed eyes. Lurking. Looming. It's there. It is always there. *He is always there.*

I'm hoping that your dad never laid an incestuous hand on you, but maybe someone else did. Someone else desecrated your beauty and Daddy did nothing about it. Another man inflicted devastation upon you and he wasn't there. Your dad wasn't around to stop it. Your dad failed to make you safe again. He was absent, but you weren't. You endured every horrible minute. He was silent. You were calling for help. You're still calling for help. *Save me. Save me, Daddy.* Still no answer.

THIS IS MY DANCE SPACE

I love to dance. It is a great way to express a little creativity, or for some of you, perhaps a whole lot of creativity! Sometimes it's just a release of stress. Not surprising, I am rather fond of the 1980s movie *Dirty Dancing*. One of the scenes I remember the most is when Patrick Swayze is instructing Jennifer Grey on her carriage, or frame. "Look, spaghetti arms. This is my dance space. This is your dance space. I don't go into yours, you don't go into mine. You gotta hold the frame." He was very particular about them staying in their own space. It was as if there was an invisible line between them that wasn't to be crossed. If the line was crossed, then somehow it ruined the beauty of the dance. Each of them had a specific role to play in their dance together. If one of them messed up, it could mean heartbreak for the other who would have to attempt to compensate for the mistake.

They had a line that should not have been crossed. The more experienced dancer already knows the line exists. He knows the unspoken rules. In life, there are lines and unspoken rules everywhere. They are what we call boundaries. Lines, or boundaries, exist in many aspects of our lives to serve as protective barriers from emotional, physical, psychological, and spiritual wounds. As children, it is our parents' job to teach us those boundaries and see to it that they are enforced. Otherwise, living in the real world would become fairly treacherous and confusing. These lessons must be taught just as any life skill — for the sake of our survival and success.

Fortunately, some boundaries are instinctual. For example, as a little girl it feels wrong for someone to snatch something out of your hands. You may not know what to do about it, but you know it is hurtful. It's one thing if kids at day care are swiping your stuff mid-play, but it's another in itself if your dad rips toys out of your hands. He's crossing your boundary with a much deeper impression. He is showing you that your feelings don't matter. When Daddy feels like taking something, you don't count. You are unimportant. Your supposedly protective daddy has just crossed an invisible line. He has violated your boundary.

In Dr. Earl R. Henslin's book *You Are Your Father's Daughter* he tells us:

> In reality, a boundary violation is an experience of abuse of the inner child. It wounds her very soul. It lowers her self-esteem and leaves her with feelings of shame, anxiety, and fear.
>
> Every boundary violation becomes a learning experience for the child that will stick with her throughout life, impacting every area of life. When a child's boundaries are violated, she learns that the world is a scary place. She receives a very confusing message and fails to learn how or where to set appropriate boundaries. She loses confidence in her identity and her ability to express her needs and desires, which leads to boundary failure later in life.[5]

Precious little ballerinas are not meant to meet any of their daddy's needs. None. No little girl was created to fulfill any of her father's desires. We were designed to crave emotional and physical closeness from our dads. It is a sweet, sweet thing to want Daddy's love and affection. It is a privilege for daddies to shower their daughters with words of love and affirmation, as well as hugs and kisses. Being in the presence of a father who loves his princess well allows for her to grow up feeling confident of her dance space.

So what happens if your father doesn't love well? What happens if he is downright horrible? What happens when Daddy crosses a boundary other than toy thievery? What happens when Daddy tramples a line so tender it destroys something inside his daughter? What happens when the man of your childhood dreams utterly assaults your dance space?

> Of all the ways a father can wound his daughter, the impact of his touch through sexual abuse is one of the most devastating. Sexual abuse is a boundary violation that destroys the soul *(You Are Your Father's Daughter)*.[6]

 64

Daddy, Do You Love Me?

Abuse destroys the soul. Not wounds, but destroys. When something is destroyed, it must be rebuilt. If you have been sexually abused by your dad, or any man who held importance in your life, I pray you have seen an amazing General Contractor. The best builder I know started out with a little bit of dirt. My prayer for you is that you go back to the dirt and rebuild this devastation in your soul.

Shelby's Thoughts

I haven't the foggiest. . . . If you read those words and your head was permeated by memories, I am overcome with sadness for you. My soul weeps for you. I cry for the little girl who was lost so long ago in a bed of unwarranted shame and confusion. No one, *no one*, should ever close their eyes and see pictures of their dad ripping away their dignity. If I could erase the memories, I would do it in a heartbeat. If my words could paint an embrace around you . . . then may it be one of compassion, of love, and shelter. May I be an extension of a much gentler embrace, a more powerful love, and a great deal stronger shoulder on which you could rest.

Your body should never have been violated — never. What's more, the body of God's daughter should never have been abused by her dad, or anyone else. The bodies we are given belong to a much better Father. He wants them to be protected and treated with love and respect. One day, the man who robbed you *will answer* for his crimes. He will stand in front of a Holy God, perhaps a righteously angry Daddy, and be confronted with no escape.

I hope that Ann's story helped you to hope if you have none. I pray that your heart can find solace under the wings of the very One who allowed your pain. "For the Lord is close to the brokenhearted and saves those who are crushed in spirit" (Ps. 34:18). It may sound unbelievable, but I know it to be true. *I know it.* And He knows you. He knows your pain. He knows if you're angry with Him . . . if you feel abandoned by Him. And He cares.

> "The LORD your God is with you, he is mighty to save. He will take great delight in you, he will quiet you with his love, he will rejoice over you with singing" (Zeph. 3:17; NIV).

God doesn't offer us a little Band-Aid and Neosporin to cover up our damaged hearts. He offers complete healing.

Ariel Allison and Shelby Rawson

His name was Johnny and I met him when I was 13. His mother had been murdered a few months earlier, and he was eager to find a woman to fill her place in his heart. My father acted as though I didn't exist and I was desperate for attention from the opposite sex. Oh yeah, my relationship with Johnny was sick and twisted on so many levels.

My father never once laid a hand on me in a sexual way, but what breaks my heart is that he stood idly by and let another man do it. As a matter of fact, he was complicit in the loss of my innocence, although completely unbeknownst to him.

Several months after I started dating Johnny, my grandfather became very ill with cancer and my mother left for three months to take care of him. During that time I stayed at home with my father so I could continue going to school. My dad attended a Bible study on Tuesday nights, and asked Johnny to come over and watch me, my brother, and my sister so we wouldn't be alone. Yeah, my dad asked my boyfriend to baby-sit me so he could go to a Bible study! My 18-year-old boyfriend to be exact.

I don't know why my father was so stunned when he found several pornographic books and magazines under my mattress a short time later. Johnny had given them to me so I could sharpen my "skills." (It still makes me want to puke just thinking about it.)

Thanks to that relationship, there are now horrible pictures of me floating around this world, in the hands of someone that my dad assumed was just a baby sitter. I have spent 14 years worried that those pictures will surface. I finally realized that what happened to me was not my fault. I should have been protected. My father should have never let that man within a hundred yards of me. I don't need to fear those pictures. The man who has them does. They are nothing less than child pornography.

My dad was not the kind of man who bought *Playboy* and kept it in the bathroom. As a matter of fact, I remember being a young child and walking into a convenience store with him. There was an article he had been wanting to read in the latest edition of *Playboy*. So we went to the counter, he paid for the magazine and then ripped the article out, leaving the magazine and its contents in the store. On one hand, there was a man of great principle, but the dichotomy occurred in other areas. He had no problem renting movies with explicit sex scenes and watching them with his family. I remember being embarrassed for him that he did not

Daddy, Do You Love Me?

skip through the scenes, and I often reminded him to do so. I was well acquainted with sex and nudity long before I left grade school. Looking back, it seems as though little or no effort was put forth to protect me from a world that I didn't need to know about.

No, my father would have never laid a hand on me in a sexual way, but he seemed perfectly willing to hand my innocence to someone else on a silver platter. And you know what? He *knew*. I don't know if he knew while it was actually happening, but he certainly knew later. He didn't say anything, either to Johnny or to me. My father knew that I had been sexually molested and he never said a single word about it to me.

It wasn't until several weeks before my father died that he asked me about those three months and he wept. The guilt of what he allowed to happen to his daughter was eating him alive. My father was never good at saying he was sorry, but that day he begged for my forgiveness. Although he didn't ask for it until the very end, I had granted it years earlier.

I just wish he had sat me down when it happened. I wish he had told me the truth about my purity, that it was a precious thing not to be squandered. I wish he had taken action against the one who stole it. It would have done my young heart so much good to be protected and fought for. Yes, he was partially at fault, but when he finally admitted it, it healed us both. That healing could have come so much sooner, and would have saved me from sexual behavior that continued for years.

Endnotes

1. John Eldridge, *Wild at Heart: Discovering the Secret of a Man's Soul* (Nashville, TN: Thomas Nelson, 2001), p. 37.

2. Dr. Earl R. Henslin, *You Are Your Father's Daughter* (Nashville, TN: Thomas Nelson Publishers, 1994), p. 23.

3. Eldridge, *Wild at Heart: Discovering the Secret of a Man's Soul*, p. 182.

4. John Cougar Mellencamp, "Jack and Diane" (Mercury/Universal records, 1990).

5. Henslin, *You Are Your Father's Daughter*, p. 62–63.

6. Ibid., p. 72.

Who's Your Daddy?

When I became a father
    in the spring of '81
There was no doubt that stubborn boy
    was just like my father's son.
    — George Strait
      "Love Without End, Amen"

All of the men in her family stand the same way. It makes no sense to her, but they all seem to take enormous pride in it. Hands on hips. Right leg straight. Left leg out to the side. Head cocked. If you have a cowboy hat and a stalk of grain to chew, even better! Being that they are all Texans sheds a little more light on it. They are citizens of Texas first and then the United States! It's in their blood. Poor guys can't help it. The pride of their homeland and intense masculine persona is imprinted on their DNA. It is who they are, and really it is a wonderful thing. Come on girls, you know you wanted to be swept off your feet by a cowboy! The Marlboro Man is the quintessential picture of the American male.

So that is where she comes from, Texas cattle ranchers and cotton farmers. You can't get more down home than that. She is a descendant of the spirit that took the West. A little Cherokee blood flows through her veins as well, which explains where she gets her whooping screech when she's angry! She knows where she comes from. She looks at family pictures and can identify the source of each feature, though they are scattered amongst relatives on both sides of her family. She has her mother's lips and her father's jaw. The temper and figure both come from her grandmother. The creativity flows through generations of artists. She's only been on a horse a handful of times, but somehow it just feels right. She laughs like a hyena, and chats like a motor boat. She knows exactly how her father has affected her DNA, and her day-to-day life. In many ways he is a replica of his own father.

WHAT IS YOUR FATHER'S STORY?

Who is your father? Not what does he do for a living or what does he look like, but who *is* he? Where was he born? What was his childhood like? What kind of relationship did he have with his parents — especially his father? Does he have any brothers or sisters? Did he have a lot of friends growing up, or was he a loner? Did something tragic happen during his life? Was he abused as a kid? Did he grow up in a single parent home? Was he the forgotten middle child? Did he have life handed to him on a silver platter, or did he grow up in a poor home, scrounging to make ends meet?

Do you have a father who was always expected to be the perfect son? Does he have a good work ethic, or is he lazy? What was his parents' relationship like? When he got disciplined as a child, what did that look like?

In case you haven't figured it out yet, this is what I am asking. Do you really *know* your father? Did he grow up in a home where he had great parents that modeled love, affection, and acceptance? Or was he raised in a dysfunctional family where abuse, insults, and rejection ran rampant? The answers to these questions really do matter. They matter to you and they matter to the relationship you have with your father today.

In so many cases, our fathers are only acting out what was modeled for them. In a lot of cases, they are actually doing a better job being a dad than their own fathers.

Why is this knowledge so important? Because you need to understand why your father parents the way he does. If he did not have

Daddy, Do You Love Me?

a strong, compassionate, noble dad full of integrity, he will not know how to be that kind of dad. He will have to learn that on purpose, and he may not want to, much less even understand that he is doing something wrong.

Perhaps his dad left his mother and so it only seemed normal for him to do that to your mom. Perhaps he was beaten every time he did something wrong as a child, so when he slapped you across the face he thought that was how he should discipline. Or maybe it isn't as extreme as that. Maybe his dad never patted him on the back and said, "Atta boy." Maybe he longed for it and never got it and so he doesn't give it to you because he doesn't know how. Maybe he was expected to excel and perform and make his dad look good, and so now he cares more about your performance than your heart.

You see, these things matter. It is so important to know why he has made the choices that he has.

It is true that some men were raised by incredibly noble parents and they simply chose to be selfish, evil jerks. It happens, but not all that often. Very rarely does a man who has been raised by a great dad turn out to be truly rotten. Not to say they don't struggle and have their own issues, but in most cases, when a man (or a woman) has truly been parented well, they try to do well by their children. They *try*.

So we aren't talking about those rare bad apples, we are talking about the ones that don't fall far from the tree. You know a tree by its fruit and there is a good chance that your family tree has some dead branches.

Since you're reading this book, I also know that there is a very tender spot inside your heart that longs to be in a different place with your dad. This is where compassion enters the scene. This is where we recognize that we have to be able to see our dads in a different light. For so long we have looked at them as the men that hurt us. We see all the damage they have inflicted and it just makes us angry. We see their mistakes, faults, neglect.

I know from experience that if you choose to only see your father in that light, your relationship will never change. Not only will it never change, it may get worse, and the condition of your heart will only spiral downhill. Yes, we do have to acknowledge our wounds, and acknowledge the one who delivered them. It is okay to go to that place emotionally and mourn. It is okay to go there, but it is not okay to stay there. Because you see, your dad isn't just your dad. He is a man. He is a husband. He

Ariel Allison and Shelby Rawson

is someone else's son. I can guarantee that if he hurt you, it is because he is hurting himself.

Because he wears more than the "Daddy" hat, we have to look at who he is in the context of everything he is. That is why it is so important to know where he came from, and what his family of origin looked like. It is important because it will help you understand, and when you understand, you can make room for compassion in your heart.

It is time to take a look at his wounds, his sorrows, and his life. We will not excuse his sin, but we will try to understand his choices and his heart.

After the last chapter, it may be very difficult for us to turn the corner and view our fathers from a different angle. We just read the remarkable and heartbreaking story of Ann Cameron. I don't know about you, but I feel sick to my stomach every time I hear about what she endured as a child. Yet I believe it would be fitting to hear from her again and see how she turned that corner in her own life. How did she learn to view a sexually abusive father through eyes of compassion?

A PATTERNED LIFE

There is nothing good in my relationship with my dad, nor will there ever be. All communication has been cut off and I still have a lingering dread of the man that violated me so terribly. For so long I feared him and I hated him. I had resigned myself to those emotions because I did not know how to escape them. It wasn't until I began to ask different questions that I found a way to release my hate. I began to look at my father as a man trapped in the bondage of serious sexual sin. To view pornography online is one thing; to rape your four-year-old daughter is something else entirely. A man capable of doing that has a profoundly corroded heart. So I began to do research on how sexual predators come into existence. Little boys don't grow up to be monsters without something terrible happening. In the vast majority of cases, they were sexually abused themselves. For those that were not, the causes are just as hideous; exposure to hard core pornography, or even child pornography.

When I began to look at my father in that light, it was sobering. There was something horrible in his life that ate away his moral core—something heinous. I have no proof, but I deeply suspect he endured the horrors of rape himself as a small boy. It begins to make sense. I finally understand how he could do that to his own daughter. The prey became the predator.

Daddy, Do You Love Me?

He was not looking at me through the eyes of a loving father, but through the eyes of a sexual predator. He never got help. No one ever walked him through his loss of innocence. No one rescued that little boy.

As he festered in his pain, he gained control by intimidating others. This perspective enables me to see my father for who he truly is — a broken, miserable man lashing out in his own pain. It gives me compassion. It does not excuse what he did to me, but it allows my heart to hurt for him, instead of just for myself. When I view my abusive father as a desecrated child, I am able to relate to him on a level I never thought I could. I know what it feels like to be desecrated, and no one — not even my father — deserves that.

What's more astounding, I have learned, is that my mother was molested when she was young. No wonder she was drawn to my father. No wonder she remained silent while he tortured her daughters. She did not know any different either! The legacy passed down to me by my parents was that of a grossly perverted version of parenting. At some point in their lives they crossed the line between being sinned against to being the sinner. Nevertheless, they chose. We all have the power to choose.

So here I am, no longer a victim, but a survivor, and it is up to me to stop that generational curse. I will protect my children, and I will give so much better to them than what I received. It stops here. The sin that has haunted my family, for who knows how many years, ends today!

To the best of my knowledge, Joe is unrepentant, and will most likely stay that way. He would just as soon kill me as speak to me. I fear his heart is past the point of redemption. I, on the other hand, have been able to forgive. I have been able to lay it aside. I do not say that I have forgotten — I haven't. Memories that were once covered in darkness and shame have been brought to the light, but they are powerless against me now because they have been laid at the feet of Christ. I am a new woman, and I am learning that God restores my life.

Through my daughters I am experiencing a childhood of wonder and delight. I bask in the love that their father showers upon them. Through God's mercy I am seeing what it feels like to have a loving father.

I now understand my earthly father, and because I do, I am free.

THE POWER OF CHOICE

Do you hear the power in Ann's voice? It is not resignation or acceptance. It is purposeful. She chose to go there. She chose to understand.

She chose mercy and forgiveness. I can think of few people in this world who would advise Ann to understand her father. Yet she knew that in knowing his story lay many of the answers she needed to understand her own.

WHO'S YOUR DADDY?

It takes effort to view our fathers as real people who may very well have experienced their own junk growing up. If you don't know your dad's story, you need to learn it. If you do know it, revisit it while walking in his shoes. Maybe he has no reasons for the way he has behaved, but maybe he does. (That's not to say you should look for excuses!) Just maybe he deserves a little tiny bit of grace. In order for you to truly know your own story, you need to start at the beginning. You can't judge a book by its cover, and you sure as heck can't start it in the middle and truly understand its message.

Like it or not, part of our dad's stories are part of us. No, I'm not saying that our story is all that we are. If that were the case, I'd be miserably depressed thinking of the label an old professor gave me. "Statistic." I should have been on drugs, or pregnant before turning 18. If I let my story define me, I would certainly be at a different place in my life today. Perhaps, if your father let his story define him, he would have beat you within an inch of your life. Maybe your dad would have come home drunk more often than not — just like his father. The point is, every person has enough history to fill the pages of a book. Each of us has at least one page — if not a thousand — we'd like to tear out and burn. Can you think of anything in your father's past that wounded him? Something that marked him deeply, but he never speaks of it?

You may have no desire to do this. It may sound like the dumbest thing you've ever heard. You know all there is to know about the man who carried your other chromosome. Do you really? Do you know everything from the outside looking in? Try looking at things from a different perspective. Look at his story as if he is just another man. (This is part of the whole "walk a mile in their shoes" bit I was giving you earlier!) Once you've done this, look at the choices he's made. Can you see any connection? Now look at your own life. I can pretty much bet you've made decisions based on things that happened to you growing up. If you're anything like me, it may have been easy to reason away your poor choices because of something that happened to you as a child.

Daddy, Do You Love Me?

MIND THE MUCK

I'm not going to sit here in a high and mighty chair telling you that you have no good reason for making the choices in your life. As I was once told, there is a reason and an excuse. I have lots of *reasons* for being defensive, standoffish, and insecure. Does that automatically excuse my behavior? Sometimes it makes it understandable, but not necessarily excusable. If you are still making excuses for yourself because of a past you had no control over, I am going to be blunt. Knock it off. Sounds harsh, I know. It probably ticked you off a little. Nevertheless, I'm not going to back down on this one. You see, I'm attempting to force you to take a step forward. Take a step out of your muck. Make a choice to move. This is *your* life now. It is no longer the life your dad set up for you.

Nope, it won't make the reasons go away. Choosing to move won't even make the behaviors take a hike, but, and there is a but, it empowers you to take responsibility for your actions. Your dad is not answerable for the choices you are making in your life today — you are. *Yes, you.* It feels so much better to point the finger at the man who caused so much pain instead of focusing on yourself. I won't blow you smoke, either. It is a process. Quite often, it is a long and messy process. For some of us in the process, there are days when it seems to be perpetual. Even so, the place we are headed is much better than the place where we were stuck.

What does this look like for you? That I cannot answer with certainty because I don't know what baggage you're lugging around these days. The first step is simple. (Notice I did not say easy!) Pretend you're in AA. "The first step to recovery is admitting you have a problem." You need to admit to yourself if there are patterns or behaviors in your life that are a little bit screwy. I'm not telling you to stand in a room full of people and do it. Take a little time to be introspective and sincerely consider your life as it stands today. Consider past relationships. Consider mistakes. Consider wounds you may have inflicted on someone else. It won't take long for patterns to show themselves and behaviors to become more obvious. So, was your dad present in every situation forcing you to make those choices? (If he was hovering over you, I am more sorry than you can imagine!)

More than likely, you have made choices as a result of your woundedness. Who hasn't affected others because of her wounds? Not me. I couldn't say that if hell froze over and pigs flew from the ice. So that puts us in the same rowboat with a leaky bottom. We need to look at the holes and

Ariel Allison and Shelby Rawson

start the patching process, but first, you need a clear view of the damage. You can't do that if you're sulking in the bottom of your boat.

Once you're able to do this, then it's possible that you may be able to see more clearly. You may be able to not only see your own life, but your father's, as well. You may be able to put him in the human category instead of the jerk/deadbeat/liar category.

Shelby's Thoughts

My Grandpa passed away on a Saturday. Funny, those are the days I would usually see him growing up. When I arrived, he would either be in his usual seat at the kitchen table or sitting with his feet up in his recliner. If he wasn't there, you could bank on the fact that he was in the fields working. He met me with his usual greeting, "Well, hi!" I can still hear his voice . . . see his glasses, jeans, shoes. He was a very constant piece of my life. I cannot recall a single time he raised his voice to me, and he always had a smooch and a smile when I left. He and the love of his life are still two of my favorite people.

Then Saturday came again. I remember the phone call — the disbelief, sitting alone on my couch sobbing. He couldn't be gone. Grandpa was supposed to live to meet my children one day. My children were supposed to meet the man I loved so much.

The trip home seemed to take forever. We were going to stay at my dad's house — which was making me a little nervous. My dad and I were rebuilding our relationship and I knew there would be time alone with him. We went to all the viewings and finally the funeral. Afterward, we talked about Grandpa and how special he was to me. Then Dad did something surprising. He put in a movie he thought I should see.

The movie was depressing. It was a very sad story revolving around father-son relationships. It was his way of showing me a little piece of my family story — from my great-grandfather to my dad . . . and, in a way, to me. That week I learned a little more about my grandpa's life growing up, but more importantly, some truths about my dad's youth. I caught more of a true glimpse into my dad's life. He showed me a page of his story.

It would have been so easy for me to ignore the new pages revealed to me. I could have refused to see them for what they were — just plain truth. After all, if I see the more human side of my father, it might make it more difficult to hang on to hurt. It would actually mean that I might

Daddy, Do You Love Me?

just be forced to realize his life wasn't all cherries. Yes, my dad knew he was loved by his father, but not because Grandpa was an affectionate and verbally affirming kinda guy. Even though my relationship with my dad seemed to be throwing lemons at me growing up, in the good times, he said he loved me and he hugged me — a step in the right direction.

As a child, I don't feel that it's possible or necessary to view our parents as just normal people who make mistakes. There is a lack of security in that. As an adult, you come to a point when you should do this. It's part of living in reality. I still don't know every page of my dad's story, but I know more now than in the past. The biggest thing I learned in contemplating his story was the place I'd held him in for so long. I wanted my dad to be my hero. I wanted him to be superman for me. I'd never considered the idea that he was just a man. He was supposed to be more than that. . . . Right?

I wanted him to be more than a man, and, rightly so. It is what we wish for as daughters. We dream of our dads being the knight on a white horse who comes to save us. So when he isn't on his steed, we don't know what to do. I didn't know how to deal with a dad who made mistakes. I didn't know how to deal with the damage done to my heart. How does a little girl protect herself from the pain caused by an imperfect man? She doesn't. Those aren't life skills they teach in school.

One clear day, I began to see him. I began to see my dad as an ordinary man. In seeing the ordinary, the extraordinary expectations start to diminish. The heavy load of misplaced hope lightens. My eyes take on a new focus. Instead of honing in on cons, I learned to look at the pros.

My dad isn't perfect. They are not going to write a book about the perfect father-daughter relationship using us as their role models! I realize that you're reading this book because your dad made his own share of mistakes. I have no idea what those mistakes have been. . . . I don't know if he beat you, ignored you, criticized you, or shamed you. Maybe he did all of the above and more.

Your dad may still be an unrepentant, hateful man. His past doesn't excuse the choices he made in your life. Having an awful past doesn't give him an "easy button" to absolve him from the scars he's given you. The reason I want you to look at your dad like any other man is for your sake — not just for his sake. You may not believe that you have him on a pedestal, but I'm guessing that somewhere in your heart that is exactly where you want him to be. Your dad may never have been given the tools he needed to be a great daddy to you. (Yes, he *should have tried* to be a better dad for you!) The cry of my heart is that you would be able to look at your dad objectively. If he was raised by wonderful parents and treated you like invisible crud, then so be it. That is the reality of the situation — and it stinks. It is another loss for you to openly recognize and grieve. If your dad was raised by abusive parents, then that is a reality as well. Again, it's okay for you to look at the hand you were both dealt and mourn.

I just want you to look! Remove the lenses of life experience and take a bird's-eye view. The emotions you have are up to you. Who is your daddy?

Ariel's Thoughts

On June 28, 2005, I got a phone call that changed my life forever. It was one of those mornings that you just muddle through. My eight month old was sitting in a pool of spit up. My toddler was playing drums on his high chair with a hairbrush and a spatula. In the midst of the chaos and noise, I was trying unsuccessfully to make scrambled eggs and pour coffee at the same time. My teeth were unbrushed and my hair was disheveled. It had all the makings of being a rotten day.

I finally found the phone under a dirty dish towel, and almost didn't answer. I didn't recognize the area code and almost passed it off as a telemarketer. But I answered anyway, and when I heard the voice on the other end of the phone, my heart stopped.

"This is Will Allison, may I speak to Ariel?"

My uncle. I can only remember seeing him once in my life, 15 years earlier. I couldn't believe he had actually called me back. While catching up on the basics, I managed to get one child down for a nap and the other situated in front of a movie so I could talk without interruption.

"Please tell me about my grandfather," I said as I plopped exhausted onto the couch.

On my father's deathbed he had made me promise that I would contact my uncle Will and have him tell me the stories about Lee Franklin Allison, my grandfather. My father had tried to tell me about this man his entire life, but I had refused to listen. I am ashamed to say that anything my father tried to tell me was immediately discarded. My failings as a daughter are many, but the one that I regret the most is simply not listening to the voice of my father when he tried to impart family heritage to me. I thought they were tall tales at the best, surely they couldn't be true. My grandfather couldn't possibly have had a run-in with Hitler, or done covert ops for General Patton, and there was no way on earth I was going to believe that he had gone toe to toe with John Wayne.

All that I knew of this man is that he had disowned my father and dismissed me with a single glance. I had spent a lifetime trying to reconcile the man of legends with the man who had barely acknowledged my existence.

When I left the message on my uncle's answering machine a week earlier, I thought that I was just fulfilling a promise I'd made to my father. I had no idea that I was about to receive a priceless gift.

In a voice full of Texas grit, and cowboy humility, my uncle told me the story of a legend. Unlike many legends, this one was true, down to the minutest detail. My father had neither lied nor exaggerated. My grandfather had indeed competed at the Olympics, won the Golden Gloves for Texas boxing, and fought in World War II and won a Bronze Star. He spoke fluent French, Italian, and German. He did capture the Lipizaner Stallions for General Patton, and he was wounded so badly in combat that he was left on the battlefield for dead. He did nearly come to blows with John Wayne on the set of *The Alamo*, only to later have a speaking role in the movie and then become friends with the man.

We talked for over two hours, and as I listened to the stories, I found myself swelling up with a sense of family pride that I had never known before. So much of my life had been spent in shame, shame of who I was and where I came from. I didn't know these stories. I didn't know I had such a heritage or so much to be proud of. I didn't know that the blood of champions ran through my veins.

Then the conversation turned to a more intimate and a more painful subject. I wanted to know why my father and my grandfather had such a terrible falling out. I wanted to know why I had never known this legend. The answer to that question did something that surprised me; it gave me compassion for my father in a way that I would have never suspected. It explained everything, right down to why he wore his old army shirts every day.

Granddad saw my father for the first time when he was four years old. He had tried to get time off for the delivery, but had to report for duty again two days before dad was born. World War II took him away from his family for four years. After a short return to his wife and son,

Ariel Allison and Shelly Rawson

the German Occupation demanded his presence, and then again during the Korean War he was gone. For all intents and purposes, my father was raised without a dad. All he had were stories, and that is what he clung to his entire life. The relationship had never been there. The time spent teaching a boy how to be a man had never happened. Combine that with poor choices on the part of my father as a young man, and prideful hearts by both men, they drifted apart until all that was left were memories of a legend, and bitter disappointments. I finally knew why my father had parented the way that he had; he just didn't know any better. His father was, by all accounts, a great and noble man, but somehow in the course of life they had simply missed each other completely.

Growing up, I used to wonder why my father wore his army shirts constantly. It used to embarrass me. Now I see that he did it because that is what *his* father wore. He was clinging to the only sense of pride and dignity that remained. I mocked him for it because I didn't understand.

Will told me something during the course of that call that I believe will change the course of my life forever. He said that he has a picture of me on my grandfather's lap. I am no more than five years old, and there is a look on my granddad's face that Will said he had never seen before or since, one of dopey delight. He was thrilled to have a granddaughter, Will told me. He loved me, Will told me. I evoked something in his heart that had never been felt before. I soaked those words up like a sponge. I had believed my entire life that I had been utterly unloved by that man. Now here I was, found to be the delight of a legend. I thought my heart would explode.

Will also told me things I never knew about my father. He told me how much he loved his brother, and how his father had never spoken an unkind word about my dad. They certainly hadn't understood one another, but Granddad loved his son. Will told me that my father had been a rodeo champion, and a military police officer who had saved countless lives. I delighted to hear of my father's exploits in Germany. I learned that he had saved the life of a man when I was a child. Neither my mother nor I had ever heard the story.

What I got that day was a piece of my heritage. I got back a sense of pride and belonging to a story bigger than myself. I got answers to why my father had been the way he was. I got the knowledge that I mattered to someone. Above all, I gained the ability to understand my father, the man who had hurt me so badly. As I think of him now, I am able to filter my memories of the man through the reality of his life. It helps me understand why he chose the life he did. I found something I feared I would never have for the man: respect. I had forgiven him, and I still loved him, but I hated that I did not respect him. I was given that, and it has changed the way I think of my father and the way I speak of him.

I cannot promise that you will find a great hero in your family if you truly try to know about your father's history, but I can promise that you will find answers. You will better understand the man who gave you life, and possibly offer compassion for his hurts.

Daddy, Do You Love Me?

And I will be a father to you,
And you shall be sons and daughters to Me,
Says the Lord Almighty
        (2 Corinthians. 6:18; NAS95).

Chapter
5

> He can't remember the times that he thought
> *Does my daddy love me?*
> Probably not.
> But that didn't stop him from wishing that he did.
> Didn't keep from wanting or worshiping him.
>   — Jimmy Wayne
>   "I Love You This Much"

She was lost in memories . . . thinking of her friend's father who was so kind. She wasn't his daughter, yet somehow he took an unfamiliar step to show her he was concerned. Their family was like a pair of old sneakers — you fit right in. No hiding. No performing. No criticizing. No hoping and wishing for love to cast a piece of its shadow on you. . . . She misses them. She misses him.

There was Tracie's dad. When things became unbearable, he offered to let her move in with their family. She couldn't believe that he was willing to just take her in — no questions, no expectations. Just to be sheltered under their roof. *He* thought she was a good daughter. The bitter pain of those days is sweetened by the gesture of Tracie's father.

In college, there were several friends who had amazingly close relationships with their dads. She watched and listened while happiness, sadness, and envy played on her heartstrings. As her teenage years drifted away, her heart began a journey of its own. For years it learned to traverse roads that protected and defended her father, taking detours for inadequacy and hitting roadblocks of performance and criticism. The shell around her emotional core was cracking. It began leaking from the torrents of hurt and unanswered questions that were once under close guard.

"Why am I not good enough?"

"Why was I never thin enough?"

"Why wasn't I his favorite?"

"Why am I such a disappointment?"

"Why doesn't he think I'm beautiful?"

"Why wouldn't he stand up for me?"

"Why doesn't he love me?"

Journals became a playground for the mental bullies to attack her again and again.

> I am a loser. My own father doesn't care about me. He cheated on my mom when she was pregnant with me. He never wanted me. He cannot stand the sight of me. Why would he? God's not supposed to make junk, but this piece slipped by Him. I am nothing but a piece of junk. I'm worthless. If I died tomorrow, no one would miss me. No one would come to my funeral.

She wonders again why her own father didn't even love her.

A TROUBLING QUESTION

Daddy, do you love me?

I am staring 30 years old in the face and that question still brings tears to my eyes. Oh, I've asked it a million times, but mostly in my head. There was one time that I stood next to a dying man and said the words out loud. I said them, and I thought it would kill me, but he was the one that died, and I sit here, years later, with that question troubling

Daddy, Do You Love Me?

me again. Yet it is not my earthly father that I wonder about. I got the answer to *that* question hours before he slipped into eternity. I wonder it of someone else entirely, someone I have never seen, someone I have never touched. I do not know what His aftershave smells like, and I have never looked in His eyes. It is a different Father that I ask that question of today, the one who claims to be a Father to us all.

"Daddy, do You love me?"

Me — this woman today, right now. Do You love me? I won't even begin to ask why You let all those things happen to me. I barely have room in my heart for the answer I need most. Do You love me? God, do You love me? Abba, do You love me? *Daddy*, do You love me?

We ask this question of our earthly fathers, but we must also ask it of our Heavenly Father. Jesus taught us to refer to God as "Abba" or "Daddy." In the context of our loss and hurt we must find the courage to approach God as our ultimate Father, and look to Him to fill the empty places in our hearts.

The following is an excerpt from Madeleine L'Engle's *Walking on Water*:

> I was told of a man who had a small son he loved dearly, and so he wanted to protect him against all the things in life which frighten and hurt. He was emphatic in telling the little boy that *nobody* can be trusted. One evening when the father came home, his son came running down the stairs to greet him, and the father stopped him at the landing.
>
> "Son," he said, "Daddy has taught you that people can not be trusted, hasn't he?"
>
> "Yes Daddy."
>
> "You can't trust anybody, can you?"
>
> "No, Daddy."
>
> "But you can trust Daddy, can't you?"
>
> "Oh, yes, Daddy."
>
> The father then held out his arms and said, "Jump," and the little boy jumped with absolute trust that his father's arms were waiting for him. But the father stepped aside and let the little boy fall crashing to the floor.
>
> "You see," he said to his son, "you must trust *no*body."[1]

L'Engle goes on to say:

Ariel Allison and Shelby Rawson

Jesus told us to call the Lord and Creator of us all *Abba*. Not only Father or Sir or Lord, but Abba — Daddy — the small child's name for Father. Not Dad, the way Daddy becomes *Dad* when the children reach adolescence, but *Daddy*, the name of trust.[2]

This is where we as daughters become crippled. The very heart and nature we were born with longs to trust, but somewhere along the way we fell crashing to the floor while our earthly father stepped aside. Whether it happened in a single moment or over the course of a lifetime, we learned not to trust our fathers, and for many of us, we learned, as that little boy did, that we cannot trust *anyone*.

ELUSIVE FAITH

It has been said that our view of our dads has a direct relationship to our view of God. It's not a new concept. I am guessing it has been around for quite a while. After all, when you think about it, it makes some sense. God is often referred to as Father, so naturally our earthbound fathers could be tied to the way we see our Heavenly Father. If I reflect on my life for just a couple of minutes, I can attest to the validity of this concept.

I know what you're thinking. We have this God, and He is said to be almighty, loving, protecting, and safe. But you probably don't believe those things to be true of Him, do you? I am not questioning whether or not you think it is possible He is good. I am asking you if you *believe* it.

Here's my thinking on it. I absolutely believe that there is one, true God. That is something of which I am certain. What's more, if you heard me speak of Him, you would suppose that I trust Him to be loving, safe, and faithful. Chances are if you came to me with a problem, I would do my best to be empathetic and encouraging while pointing you to this Heavenly Father. I can say this honestly because I have no doubt that He will give you the best He has to offer. He will provide you with whatever you need and more. He will surpass your expectations. He will surprise you with great blessings. That's right, *you*. Are you following my thought process on this? Not once did I say He would do this for me. I said I have faith that He would do it for you. Therein lays the rub.

You may be thinking to yourself, "If she feels that way, then she must not really believe." Guess what. You are almost correct. I can logically tell you what I know to be true about God because I do believe it in my head. However, there is a connection that is missing in that statement. The belief that I need to possess must also penetrate my heart. If you know something to be true, but don't seem to have experienced it first-hand, then there is a weakness, or shakiness, surrounding it. It's kind of like watching your friend free-fall from a bungee cord and land safely. You know that the cord held her and she survived without a scratch. In spite of this, you're not so sure that cord will support you, or if the mat will stay inflated. It doesn't matter what other people tell you because there is hesitancy in your heart telling you that good and safe things don't always happen for you. They happen for other people, sure, but not for you.

This is why hope and faith can be such elusive things. Somewhere along the way, you had hopes for your relationship with your dad. Then, somewhere you invested a little faith in him, and both were dashed again and again. You began to learn a distorted lesson on hope and faith. Your connection, or lack thereof, to your father squelched your eagerness to believe in these words. So in your heart, you replaced them with another four-letter word — fear. Along with the fear you grabbed on to distrust. That fear and distrust gave you the impression you could be safe; guarded by walls of self-preservation.

At the same time, your soul propelled you onward at different times, allowing you to have hope and faith for your friends. Your friends could have great things happen for them. Your friend could have the career of which she dreamed. Another friend would marry the man of her dreams and live a successful, happy life. Would these things happen for you? You thought about it, but you didn't dare put any hope in it. You've already learned that lesson. Hope is for suckers . . . or people who've never walked in your shoes.

This attitude seems to help so much when a disappointment comes along because you've already taken steps to prepare yourself for the worst. Whew. You knew that something bad was going to happen sooner or later. You're just relieved to know that you were prepared. It doesn't mean there wasn't any hurt. It just means that you'll lower your expectations — again.

How, for the love of Pete, could anyone with this outlook believe that there is a God who is a perfect Daddy? That would require hope. That would demand faith. Youch. Are you kidding? Those happy little words are much too unreliable for a little girl who discovered the hard way that you can't put your trust in anybody — especially someone calling himself your Father.

Ariel Allison and Shelby Rawson

Still, deep down, in the far corners of your being, you know. *That is how I know.* My heart refuses to deny that He is God. He is God the Father. He created me in my mother's womb out of love for a daughter yet to be seen by human eyes. Just as He did for me, He also did for you. Life lessons from your dad may keep you from going there with your heart, but it's true. In the lessons of life, there is a God who desperately wants to teach lessons of love. He knows that it will be hard for us to understand. Just as He knows it will seem almost impossible to wrap our arms around the idea that God is a wonderful Daddy who wants the best for us. He knows it will seem almost impossible for us to move this knowledge from our heads to our hearts.

So we wrestle. We wrestle with the idea that the God who allowed junk brings joy. Not just for everyone else, but for me *and you.* I cannot pretend to know all the answers as to why God allows daughters that He loves so deeply to hurt so much, but I can tell you I know why you may find it so very hard to accept the fact that He loves you. I know because I have been that daughter. *I am that daughter.* Yet, I am also the little girl whose heart has been unearthed by gentle hands, wooing me into His ever-present shelter. I am learning that while His shelter may not shut out hurt and sorrow, it is abounding in grace, comfort, love, and peace. Don't you want peace in your shattered spirit? Don't you want rest from the burden you're carrying on your shoulders? I know your back is breaking. Your legs are tired of supporting the weightiness of fear, anger, and bitterness. Yet I imagine they are just strong enough to fall at His feet. Maybe, just maybe, your legs are anticipating the opportunity to run to a Daddy whose arms are made to embrace His little girl.

HE IS NOT SAFE

I believe that there are things that God plants in our hearts, sometimes from an early age, to give us a point of reference, a hope, something to cling to. This happened to me as a child while reading *The Lion, the Witch, and the Wardrobe* by C.S. Lewis.

Lucy has wandered into the magical world of Narnia where animals talk and anything can happen. This world is in a state of constant winter, always winter but never Christmas. It is held captive by the evil White Witch Jadis, but something is happening. Something is changing. The King, the great Lion Aslan, is returning. Aslan is on the move. So Lucy

Daddy, Do You Love Me?

asks her dear friend Mrs. Beaver a question that has haunted my life since I was five years old, "Is he safe?"

As I pondered the question of Lucy recently, my own question, in fact, I ran across the words of Renee Altson, author of *Stumbling Toward Faith*, and they leapt off the page and right into my heart. Yes, this is what I feel. This is it exactly!

> I'm reading "*The Lion, the Witch, and the Wardrobe*" to my eight-year-old daughter.
>
> She is physically eight years old, but mentally and emotionally she's still about three or four. A little young for the book, and certainly too young for the movie, but I want her to know and share in the magic and wonder that Narnia brought to me as a little girl.
>
> I grew up in an abusive environment, and the Narnia books were my refuge. I sought doorways to that world, hoping beyond hope that I, too, was destined to be a Queen. Hoping that somewhere under my bed or behind my shower curtain was a place where I was safe. A lion who could soak my tears up in his mane, and hold me with his heavy, velvet paws.
>
> I envied Lucy's magic elixir, wanting something that would heal the grief and brokenness in my heart.
>
> Tonight, I read my favorite passage to my daughter.
>
> "*Then he isn't safe?*" said Lucy.
>
> "*Safe?*" said Mr. Beaver, "*don't you hear what Mrs. Beaver tells you? Who said anything about safe? Course he isn't safe. But he's good.*"
>
> In my search for Jesus, I have struggled with this idea of good. Is God really good? How can we explain the terrible things in the world and balance them against the notion of a good God? How can a good God allow such evil?
>
> And I've definitely struggled with safe. After a lifetime of abuse and cowering and hiding, I want to feel safe. To feel like I can breathe. To know that I am beyond harm.
>
> The idea that Jesus isn't safe, but good, brings tears to my eyes. I want so desperately to truly know this. To rest in that goodness.
>
> I believe, help my unbelief.[3]

Yes, He is good — safe, no. The road is dark and dangerous and the pain immense, but oh, He is SO good. Aslan *is* on the move, in my life and in yours. The journey set before us is not placed in an English garden full of roses and fountains, but in the frozen wasteland of Narnia. We are broken and bruised from the trek, but there is hope. Spring is coming. The ice is melting. Aslan is on the move, and that great lion, son of the Emperor Beyond the Sea, loves the daughter that shivers from the cold.

NEVER BEEN UNLOVED

Is God really equipped to deal with my pain? That is the question that resonates in our hearts. Will He really be able to heal all the broken pieces of my soul? Do I even want Him to try? I have lost so much that I don't even know where to start. I don't know what it feels like to have a father. I don't know what it feels like to be loved like that . . . but I want to. In my heart of hearts I want to.

If God is truly my Father, not just my Father but my "Daddy," my Abba, then do I have the courage to ask the question my soul longs to hear, "Daddy, do You love me?" What if He says no? I can't face that kind of rejection again. I have heard so often that God loves me, but how do I really know? How can I really believe?

> I have been unfaithful,
> I have been unworthy,
> I have been unrighteous,
> And I have been unmerciful.
>
> I have been unreachable,
> I have been unteachable,
> I have been unwilling,
> And I have been undesirable.
>
> Sometimes, I have been unwise.
> I've been undone by what I'm unsure of,
> But because of you, and all that you went through
> I know that I have never been unloved.
>
> I have been unbroken,
> I have been unmended,
> I have been uneasy,
> And I've been unapproachable.

Daddy, Do You Love Me?

I've been unemotional,
I've been unexceptional,
I've been undecided,
And I have been unqualified.

Sometimes, I have been unwise,
I've been undone by what I'm unsure of,
But because of you, and all that you went through,
I know that I have never been unloved.

Unaware, I have been unfair.
I've been unfit for blessings from above.
But even I can see the sacrifice you made for me
To show that I have never been unloved.[4]
— Michael W. Smith
Never Been Unloved

So how is it that I *know* I am loved by this ultimate Father? The answer to that question lies unequivocally on the cross of Jesus Christ. We must take a closer look at that cross and realize that it wasn't a single event in ancient Israel. It is living and breathing and pertains to my everyday sin, and my deepest wounds. That cross was for me, and it was for you. It was also for your father. It was for everything your father has ever done to wound or disappoint you. God was not standing idly by while you were being hurt; He was actively righting the wrong.

GOD SPEAKS

We were born to be daughters of the King. We have been asked to call God "Daddy." We have been asked to trust. We have been asked to love. We have been asked to throw ourselves with reckless abandon into the arms of the ultimate Father. Yet we don't really believe that He will catch us. There is a part of our very souls that so badly wants to trust, so very badly wants to be *caught* in arms that will not drop us, but hold us close . . . protect us . . . caress us . . . love us.

It is true that we were meant to know, love, and relate to the man who gave us life. There is no one to replace him, and there never will be, but we aren't looking for a replacement. We are looking for truth and answers and hope. We, my friends, are looking for *love*. (Dare I say, in all the wrong places?)

Ariel Allison and Shelby Rawson

Our soul screams the question, "Daddy, do You love me?" but what is the answer? Let us hear that from our Father himself. Let us see what God has to say:

I have loved you with an everlasting love (Jer. 31:3; NIV).

I am your Provider (Matt. 6:25–33, paraphrased).

Fear not, for I have redeemed you; I have called you by name, you are mine (Isa. 43:1; RSV).

Do not be anxious about anything (Phil. 4:6; NIV).

I will bless you and make you a blessing (Heb. 6:14, paraphrased).

I will give you good gifts (Matt. 7:11, paraphrased).

I will teach and instruct you. I will guide you with my eye (Ps. 32:8, paraphrased).

Nothing that is good will be withheld from you (Ps. 84:11, paraphrased).

There is nothing too hard for You (Jer. 32:17; NKJV).

You will dwell in my house forever (Ps. 23:6, paraphrased).

Trust Me, I will not fail you in any way (Deut. 31:6, paraphrased).

And I will be a father to you, And you shall be sons and daughters to Me, Says the Lord Almighty (2 Cor. 6:18; NAS95).

Rest in my love (John 15:9, paraphrased).

With Me all things are possible (Matt. 19:26, paraphrased).

Oh, and the heart longs to go there, to believe what this Father says. It longs to be delighted in, provided for, protected, and loved. It longs deeply, but with that longing comes the fear that experience has taught us. Before we trust, before we believe, we want to know if this Father is good, if this Father is safe. The answers to those questions are simple. He is good, but He is not safe. Our own experiences have taught us that He is not safe.

Daddy, Do You Love Me?

That is the problem we face in approaching God with our broken hearts. We are to trust, wholly and completely, but at the same time we know that God is not a puppet on a string, nor is he a short order cook. He will do whatever He wants to do, whenever He wants to do it, in order to grow our faith. We know at the end of the day that He has the ultimate culpability for our broken hearts. He gave us our fathers, and He could have stopped the pain they inflicted in our lives. Yet He chose not to. He allowed every bit of it to happen, and He did not intervene. The question we must answer is whether or not we can believe that it was ultimately for our good and for His glory. He is not safe, but He is good.

No, God may not be safe, but His goodness is in abundant supply. His hands will never harm you. His hands are made for healing. His hands are made for holding. So He waits. *He waits for you*, and you may not know it, but you are waiting for Him, too.

> Out of the depths I cry to you, O LORD; O Lord, hear my voice. Let your ears be attentive to my cry for mercy. . . . I wait for the LORD, my soul waits, and in his word I put my hope. My soul waits for the Lord more than watchmen wait for the morning, more than watchmen wait for the morning (Ps. 130:1–6; NIV).

There is an innate desire we were given as women. Not today or yesterday, but long ago when we were being knit together in our mothers, this desire was there. You cannot shake it. You cannot curse it away. It won't leave. Yearning to know what it feels like to be daddy's little girl is a part of you. It is engrained in every fiber of your being. You were created to be a daddy's girl. What you need to realize is this: The amazing Daddy you long for has been with you from the beginning. He gave you life, and He will give life to your crumbled heart again. Abba Father, Daddy, God. . . . The Daddy of all your broken days wants to be the Daddy of your healing.

You can hope. You can put your hope in Him. Throw off fear. Take courage. Your Daddy has the healing in His hands for you, His little girl.

> I've been known before I was a twinkle in my mother's eye.
> I've been loved, just because, He took pleasure in my life.
> Made in secret, formed by hands

Ariel Allison and Shelby Rawson

That would one day take a nail,
He looked upon this woman
And made me, knowing I would fail.

That friends, is the story of our lives. That is the truest depth of love, of acceptance. That is the ultimate devotion, that the God of heaven and earth created us, knowing all of our junk, before we even had it.

So, in the depths of our souls, we cry out, and sometimes we whisper the question that we so desperately need to know; "Daddy, do You love me?" God, Abba, Aslan, *Daddy*, screams the answer from the edge of eternity, His eyes brimming with tears. "Yes," He says. The answer, our answer, is a resounding "YES! I have loved you before the foundations of the world. I have known your name since before time."

DADDY'S HANDS
Dian's Story

Daddy's hands were soft and kind when I was cryin'.
Daddy's hands were hard as steel when I'd done wrong.
Daddy's hands weren't always gentle
But I've come to understand,
There was always love in Daddy's hands.
— Holly Dunn
"Daddy's Hands"

After 24 years I can still close my eyes and see his hands: big hands, strong hands, able hands, tender hands, safe hands. Is it any wonder that I so easily close my prayers almost unfailingly with the phrase "In the name of the Lord Jesus, the same One whose arm has not been shortened and whose hand is mighty and able to save!"

One of my earliest memories is watching my daddy walk into the yard after work, easing up to me as I eagerly held out my latest find to him, a tarantula, and his hand, taking "my prize" into his own. As I said; big hands, strong hands, able hands, tender hands, safe hands.

I was the apple of my daddy's eye and he was my *daddy!* I was certain he could do anything and everything. His quiet, steady, unconditional love was the perfect counterpart to my fireball give-me-the-chance-and-I'll-run-the-show mother. I knew I was valued and loved. However, I also knew that his first love was my mother. What a wonderful gift for a daddy to give his daughter! Somehow, their love for God, then their great love for one another, then their love for me was just right, just as it should be. Daddy had a way of including me in his expressed love for my mother. He would quietly come in from working outside when it was cold. Mother would most often be standing at the sink or the stove, deep in dinner preparation. He would put his finger on his lips to shush me, his eyes would twinkle, he would grin mischievously, encouraging me to join the conspiracy. Then he would run his cold hand up the back of Mother's dress and wait for her to shout "Gerald Wilson!" as Daddy and I fell on the floor laughing. As she got turned fully around he would grab her and give her a resounding kiss, a "movie kiss" if you know what I mean, and wink at me over her shoulder. Ahh, I was loved, his wink said, because he loved her *so* much.

We would hold hands, or skip, or hop on one foot, or race from one cross street to the next. When I least expected it, Daddy would scoop me up and swing me up on his shoulders. I was the princess and he was my mighty steed. Laughing we would go.

The hands that held me fast and sure could also love enough to pop my behind if I ran ahead into the street. Then they would pat and comfort as he would hunker down in front of me, dry my tears, and tell me he loved me too much to let me hurt myself by breaking the rules about looking both ways before you cross.

Daddy *loved* to sing and had a beautiful voice. He always sang to me — always. I learned to love the wonderful music of the '30s and '40s because he sang that music to me. I would stand on the top of his feet as he would "dip and sway" me across the room, crooning love songs to my mother. He loved hymns. He taught me the beauty and truth of songs of faith, and he loved to sing WITH me. The first time we sang together in church I was no more than six or seven. I stood on three wooden coke boxes. I could judge how much I had grown since the last time we sang by the number of coke boxes needed. Once I began to play the piano, we would spend hours, seated side by side on the piano bench, singing our hearts out.

Daddy had these eyes that sort of crinkled when he grinned, even more so when he really got tickled. My granddaughter Madelynn has those same eyes. (Is it any wonder I call her "heart of my heart"?) They were very expressive eyes. I loved doing things that made those eyes crinkle and dance. More often than not, Mother had to really talk and gesture and threaten to get through to me, but Daddy only had to look at me. The older I got, the more I watched those eyes. I made choices and looked to those eyes. I loved him so much that I did not want to see disappointment or sadness because of things I said or did. I never, for one moment, ever doubted his love for me! His eyes reflected what his heart was feeling. Once I left home for college and beyond, when I had difficult choices to make, I would close my eyes and think about what I thought Daddy's eyes would say, and more often than not, make the right choice.

Daddy was a man of his word. He never disciplined in haste or anger or without warning, but once I was warned, he expected the warning to take.

I could sometimes "work" him, as daughters can do to daddies, but the one place that had no give was how I treated my mother. There, he held fast, no leeway, no slack. At age 13, I entered the "who-are-you-you-must-be-the-dumbest-woman-not-to-mention-mother-in-the-whole-world" stage. I got one warning. "Stop! Give your Mother the honor and respect due her. You will not speak to her like that again." For some reason, I suppose the abject stupidity of a 13 year old, I didn't heed the warning. Extending grace, he gave me one more chance. Rebellion won out again. Thus began the most painful period of my growing up. Daddy sat me down and told me that because I had chosen to disregard his warning, not once but twice, that he and I would have no conversation until he had seen a complete and extended heart change toward my mother. Well, I was dumbfounded! What did he mean no conversation? He replied that the meaning was pretty clear. Anything that needed to be said by him to me would go through Mother, but he would not be talking to me. He made it very clear that he had not raised a child to treat his wife, my mother, in such a way; therefore, until the time he could see a true and durable change, he was done talking to me.

Drastic? Yes! For every child by every daddy in such a circumstance? No! For this daughter and this daddy? Oh, yes! He told me in later years that if I thought that was a hard time, that I had no idea. As an adult and a mother, I know that it was harder on him than it was on me. The moratorium on talking lasted for several months. The first month I was sure I could just wait him out. I was wrong! The second month I thought I could bat my eyes, snuggle up, tell funny stories, treat Mother nice on occasion (the occasion being when he was watching!), say I was sorry a lot. I was wrong — and into the third month I went without my daddy, my boon companion, my singing partner, my hero. It finally began to

Daddy, Do You Love Me?

sink into my teenage brain that he meant business and that if I wanted our relationship healed and restored I would have to begin by working on my relationship with Mother. So I did. I hoped that after the first week he would see how earnestly I was trying and that he would relent. I was wrong! He waited for several weeks, watching and listening, in lots of situations, until he was sure that my heart toward Mother had really changed. When he finally broke the silence, I was in heaven! It was the best homecoming ever. He told me how he had seen me go from a rebellious, sassy teenager, disrespecting and dishonoring her mother to a young woman learning to control her tongue and finding ways to love and build a strong relationship with her mother. He told me that he knew of no better way to cause me to get serious about this problem and find ways to solve it. He told me how much he loved me. The funny thing is that as painful and hard and long (at least to me!) it was, I always knew he loved me — and that he was loving me well.

AND THE HEART SAYS "DADDY"

Did you hear the words in her story . . . Daddy . . . Daddy . . . DADDY! Not Dad, or my father, but Daddy; a child's word for love and safety. Daddy — a word I can't remember using. For me it was always, *"Daaadd!"* Even writing it, I can hear my adolescent disrespect. Or sometimes, even worse, "Yes, *F*ather," my emphasis on the "F," as though I really wanted to use a different word altogether. Oh, yes, I used them. He taught them to me.

Perhaps that is not the way you remember your daddy's hands at all. You may remember hands that struck out at you in anger, or even worse, hands that came after you sexually. Those are your memories and you hate them, but something stirs in your heart when you read Dian's story. Part of what you feel is immense anger, and the other part is intense longing. It is okay to feel those things. It is okay to remember the hurt. It is okay to embrace the longing. It is okay.

So now we know they're out there. Yes, it may be hard for us to believe at times, but there is no denying that there are some pretty great dads in this world. Your dad may not have scored so high on a scale of one to ten, but maybe you know someone who did. Maybe if given categories, your dad scored higher in some areas and super low in others.

The point of looking at a dad who got it right is not to remind you just how wrong your dad may have been — or may be. It helps just to see

Ariel Allison and Shelby Rawson

a better way of being a dad . . . to see a dad who brought out the beauty and strength in his daughter. It is important to get a grasp on the makings of a good father because it affects our choices and our decisions — particularly in relating to men. Here's a simple illustration. If you want to buy a horse, you need to know what a horse looks like. Otherwise, you might be saddled with an ass. In watching and listening to other fathers, we gain a sense of how we should be treated as women. It allows us to realize that a lot of those cruddy thoughts we have believed about ourselves may not necessarily be true. That alone can bring some healing to our hearts.

Maybe this chapter just stirred up anger and ticked you off even more at your dad. I hope not, but if it did, that's okay. I would love for you to read her story and maybe grieve a little for what you missed. I'm not telling you to get down and wallow in self-pity.

As little girls growing up we long for a hero . . . a champion. We want a daddy who rides in to rescue us when we're hurting, who stands up for us when we're pushed down, and cradles us in his arms when we cry. After all, we are princesses deep down in the dungeons of our hearts. Isn't that a little what it feels like? Instead of the castle and your knight, you got locked away in the dungeon. There is part of you that is still waiting for someone to break down the castle doors and find you in your shadowy place. Before you embrace your knight — whoever he may be — wouldn't it be advantageous to know what a true hero looks like?

What you feel when you read her story is the nudging of your true Father. He is stroking your heart and whispering that He is all that and more. He is the best Dad there could ever be.

Let us understand to a greater degree what a daddy is supposed to be, and how a daddy is supposed to lead his daughter's heart to something greater, something beyond himself.

BEST DAD IN THE WORLD

As I have explored this area of my life, and grieved the loss of my father's love, I began searching the Bible to find an example of a healthy father-daughter relationship. I made a remarkable discovery — there isn't a single story in Scripture about a father that loved his daughter well. At first I was shocked and then I became irritated. It bothered me that the God of the universe didn't include that in His Word. We know great fathers exist because we just read about one, and I'm sure they existed back then as well.

In the midst of my frustration I was reminded of several things. First of all, I realized that Scripture does include something very important. It tells us at length how God feels about wounded women. It tells us about the restoration that He brings to their lives. In a day and time where women were utterly ignored and totally belittled, it speaks volumes that the names and deeds of so many women are indelibly recorded on the pages of the Bible. We aren't talking about Susie Homemaker and Little Miss Church Goer, either. We are talking about some earthy and gritty women. Sinners. Prostitutes. Widows. Broken. Abandoned. Infertile. Hurting. Desperate. Lonely. Women just like us.

We learn about Tamar, a woman twice widowed and rejected, who by faith took her future into her own hands. Her life was one of utter rejection. She was cast away by every man in her life until God intervened.

We have Rahab, the harlot who was mercifully plucked from the devastation of Jericho because of her faith. Not only was her life redeemed from prostitution, she later married a godly man and became the great, great grandmother of King David. We can take a single glance at her life and know with fairly good certainty that she probably had an unspeakable childhood. We know the culture she lived in and we know the choices she made with her life.

Then we have a Gentile woman named Ruth. She was widowed and barren. She was an outcast of society that was protected, loved, and later married to one of the most upstanding figures in all of Scripture, Boaz. Surely it was no coincedence that Rahab was Boaz's mother. He knew about mercy and he knew how to extend it. He covered Ruth's life with mercy.

They aren't the most predictable or savory characters in the Bible, but they are three of the women in the line of Christ. There are a multitude of other lives that we can learn from: Queen Esther; Mary, the mother of Jesus; Mary Magdalene, the prostitute. I wish grace were a color we could see because the lives of these women were painted with it.

It is very interesting to note that many of the women Scripture reveals were stuck in the bondage of sexual sin. It is impossible to miss how gentle and merciful the God of heaven is in dealing with that particular sin. Compare that to how God deals with the Pharisees and religious leaders of the day. There is something incredibly tender and compassionate in the heart of God when it comes to sexual sin, perhaps because He knows the horrors that drive us there. Regardless, it only takes a brief look at Scripture to know that God has open arms for wounded women.

Ariel Allison and Shelby Rawson

That leads to the second thing that I realized in search of the perfect father-daughter relationship. I realized that it was there the entire time, only I am the daughter and God is the father. I wonder if He wanted to make it loud and clear that there is no earthly father that will not fail us at times. There is only one perfect Father. No other man will never sin against His daughter, never crush her spirit, or never wound her in some way. The entirety of the Bible is a single love letter to His daughters. He does not want us to compare our dads to some ancient figure in Scripture, but to the lover of our souls, Creator of heaven and earth.

The frustration I felt in search of that story was laid to rest when I realized that I have been given the perfect blueprint. When I am failed, hurt, rejected, or ignored, I can turn my heart back to the only true Father that I have. My earthly father was never meant to meet all my needs. He could have been the most perfect dad ever to walk this planet and my heart would have still longed for something more. My heart would have still longed for my Heavenly Father, and that is how it was always meant to be. God gives us fathers, not to complete us, but to turn our hearts to himself.

It is true that they are supposed to reflect His love for us, and sometimes they don't, but ultimately they are meant to point us toward our real Father, the Father who has always, 100 percent of the time, gotten it right.

Ariel's thoughts . . .

When a friend asked how I was feeling a couple of days after my father died, my answer was "relieved." I wasn't glad that he had passed away, but it was much easier to say, "My father is dead," than it was to say, "I go once a week and watch him die."

For six months I had been going to his home once a week. We would sit in the living room and talk, sometimes about important things, but mostly just about anything. He had this frustrating habit of only wanting to talk about what he wanted to talk about. All efforts to change the subject were futile. So I spent countless hours hearing about the war in Iraq and any number of other such subjects. I hated it. I wanted to talk about us. I wanted to talk about things that mattered, but he would have none of it. He didn't believe he was going to die.

Yet, the most agonizing part of my visits would come just as I was leaving. I would hug my father and say, "I love you, Dad."

Daddy, Do You Love Me?

"Yeah," was his only response. He *never* said it back.

Perhaps I could have found a way to live with that. Perhaps it wouldn't have hurt as badly if he hadn't been able to say it to my sister either.

My beautiful sister.

The one with his sky-blue eyes.

Abigail.

The one whose name means, "Father's delight."

On those days the departure looked like this:

Abby would hug Dad first.

"Bye, Daddy."

"Goodbye, little blue eyes," his pet name for her from birth.

"I love you, Daddy."

"I love you, too."

I would hug my dad.

"Goodbye, Daddy."

"Bye."

"I love you, Daddy."

"Yeah."

The worst four letter word in the English language.

Week after week, that is all I heard. Abby and I would talk about it in the car on the way home. Why couldn't he say it? Why didn't he love me? Maybe if I had those blue eyes. Mine were brown. Maybe if I had her pretty blonde hair. Mine was mousy brown. Maybe, just maybe . . . no, not ever.

My husband held me at night while I cried.

I wanted to scream at my father. I wanted to stop the visits. I could take his dying emaciated body more easily than I could take his rejection. Even the smell of cancer was more palatable than his coldness.

In the deepest recesses of my heart, I felt that I must press onward. I knew he would never volunteer those words to me. I knew I had to ask him, but I shouldn't *have* to ask him. I shouldn't even have to wonder if he loved me. Isn't that what daddies are supposed to do, make their daughters feel loved?

Two weeks before Thanksgiving I reached my limit. His hospice nurse said that he would more than likely not survive the week. In my mind I saw myself standing over his tombstone, asking the question that I hadn't found the courage to ask while he was alive. I didn't want that. What if the answer was "no"? Could I live with that answer? I didn't have a choice.

Ariel Allison and Shelby Rawson

Abby and I made our usual weekly visit. We sat and talked about Iraq, dead Texan writers, and the nutritional benefits of raw carrot juice. After several hours, we rose to go home. As usual, Abby went first.

"Goodbye, Daddy."

"Goodbye, little blue eyes."

"I love you, Daddy."

"I love you, too."

My turn. Slow motion.

God, my tongue feels like cotton.

"Goodbye, Daddy." My voice cracking.

"Bye."

"I love you, Daddy."

"Yeah."

The room is spinning.

I think I'm going to be sick.

Run!

Just run out that door. You don't want to know the answer to this question. Surely not knowing is better than the truth. He doesn't love you. You are not your father's delight. Abby is.

No.

I have to know.

I need to know.

"Can I ask you a question, Dad?"

He doesn't say anything, but just looks at me as he lays in that bed, barely able to lift his head from the pillow.

Tears are running down my face before I even open my mouth to speak. My heart is pounding so hard that I can hear it in my ears. I feel dizzy. The room is spinning. Then the words tumble out in a stuttering mess.

"Every time I leave, I tell you that I love you, but you never say it back. Why don't you say it, Dad?" Choking back tears. "Do you love me?"

His expression crumbles. I have touched a raw nerve. He begins to weep. "I'm sorry," he breathes. "I'm sorry I haven't said it. I do love you."

The rest is a blur. I don't remember leaving his room or walking out of the house. I don't remember how I got home that day. My only memory is that of utter relief at the knowledge that I was loved, and profound sadness for having convinced myself that I didn't need his love. It was so obvious now that I did.

Daddy, Do You Love Me?

Teenagers express fatherneed in yet more complex ways, competing with their father and confronting his values, beliefs, and of course, limits. For so many sons and daughters, it is only at the death of their father that they discover the intensity and longevity of their fatherneed, especially when it has gone begging.[5]

— Kyle Pruett
Fatherneed

Two weeks later we were all gathered in his room on Thanksgiving night. The tears flowed freely from everyone present. We had gathered to say goodbye. It was the first time since he had been diagnosed with cancer that he had admitted he was going to die. His eyes were glassy and his speech slurred as he tried to communicate to his wife, children, their spouses, and his grandchildren how much he loved them. My dad glanced around the room looking each of his children in the eyes. He had special words for everyone present. I was last in line.

He reached over and took my hand. His words are forever branded on my mind. "I delight in you, too," he said. "I do love you. I'm sorry I wasn't able to say it."

He never told me why. He never explained what it was about me that tied his tongue. I think it was because he and I had more relational issues than any of his other children. I caused him the most grief. I needed him the most and I think it terrified him.

I left the room that night knowing I would never see him again and I didn't, but before we made our way home in the rain he gave me the most precious gift I have ever received. He gave me a glimpse of what heaven will look like. He showed me a piece of God's heart toward me.

Dad knew that he would die in a few hours. He knew that once he fell asleep he would drift off into a coma never to wake again. He asked us to sing him some Christmas carols. We did. He asked us to sing his favorite hymns, starting with the old bluegrass "I'll Fly Away." We did. He prayed with us and we wept. Then he took communion with his family. His final gift to me was leading me in worship. He led me to the foot of the Cross and reminded me that I am loved. My Father loves me, loves me so much that He died for me. I *am* my Father's delight.

The next morning he was able to mutter a few words to my mother before taking his final nap. He slipped away quietly a few hours later. Those sitting by his bedside didn't even know.

Six months earlier, I would not have thanked God for breaking my heart. I learned that night, "He has wounded us, but He will bandage us" (Hos. 6:1; NAS95). Somehow He had given me the courage to place my heart in His hands, and in the process allowed me to love my father unconditionally. Much of our relationship was never discussed or fixed. I still bear the scars of a wounded woman. I still desperately want to be daddy's little girl. I never got that, but I did get something just as valuable. I was given the ability to forgive. I was given a glimpse into the heart of God, to truly know how I have wounded Him, to receive His forgiveness, and pass that on to the one who wounded me.

These days when I think of my father, I think of that Thanksgiving night. I remember how much I have to be thankful for. My life looks a lot different than it used to. I am married with two small boys, and I long to have a daughter. God in His wisdom gave me the father He did, and with my father, He allowed my pain. God in His sovereignty gave me a husband who so deeply understands what happens when a daddy disengages from his daughter. My husband walked with me through the darkest season of my life. I thank God for that season because I know that when I have a daughter she will never have to ask, "Daddy, do you love me?"

Shelby's Thoughts

Hmmm. . . . I think there is a deep part of me that has been afraid to even contemplate this idea. It almost feels wrong. I don't know, maybe a little impossible? I'm a grown woman. What does being daddy's little girl have to do with my life now?

That must be the outside of this onion talking! You know which layer I mean. I am referring to that crackled layer on the outside that keeps the onion from bringing tears to your eyes. Once that layer is gone . . . Bam! Grab the tissue! Here come the tears. I have only to peel a little of my outer shell back to reveal the truth. *I have always wanted to be daddy's little girl.*

I can still remember days of disgust. At some of my low points I would look at myself in the mirror and be encompassed by a heavy blanket of feelings — bitterness, anger, sadness, rage, and hate. Why, why, why did I have to bear the resemblance of a man who had no appreciation for my reflection? It made me so angry. There it was . . . another reminder of a painful relationship staring me in the face. I couldn't escape it. One more way for me to feel like the antithesis of beauty. I hated it. Yet I couldn't get rid of that blanket. Some days it hung on me like it was made of wool and drenched in mud. Other days it was more like a sheet.

I didn't know how to take that stupid blanket off. So, I accessorized. (Hey, what can I say? I'm a fashionable girl.) Hmmm. . . . Let's see. What goes with an underlying coat of crud? Throw up a few hundred walls of defensiveness. After all, those defenses are a lot like shoes. You need new ones for different situations. What else? Oh, yes. Who can have all this without a good scarf of criticism wrapped snuggly around one's neck? (That makes it easier to beat yourself up. Just start by choking your own neck with self-criticism!) My heart also made its home on my sleeve on many occasions. This allowed for my low self-esteem to be starved more easily. Brilliant, don't you think?

My "blankie" started sleeping with me, too. When that happened, the blanket was able to rest comfortably and get cozy. All the while it began suffocating me and forcing more tears and questions in the middle of the night. *Why, God? Why am I losing sleep over this? Why is it that I can list off accomplishments and still feel utterly worthless? Why does he still think I'm worthless? I am nothing. Can't You please take me home with You so I don't wrestle in pain any longer? Haven't tears stung my eyes long enough?* That's how my restless nights would be. It was much better this way, because no one else had to deal with my junk. Just me — oh, and my blankie.

I wanted to understand why God would give me a dad who didn't seem to care if I was alive. I tried so hard to get his attention . . . his approval . . . a little affirmation. It seemed the only thing that could gain notice was a falling grade or a money situation.

I can still remember being curled up in the corner of my bed when I was a sophomore in high school. Report cards had just arrived and I didn't do so well in chemistry. (Probably because I was heavily involved in extracurricular activities, not to mention taking algebra II and geometry with no study hall period — all at the same time.) It didn't matter that my average was still an A-, or that I was doing well in everything else. The fact is that I can barely get myself to write the grade on paper because to this day I am still disgusted and embarrassed by it. I am literally feeling anxious right now. Okay. I'm going to spill it. I got a C+ in that stupid class. I am still mortified. So, you may be able to guess that I wasn't feeling too great at that time about my first C.

I was in my room when the phone rang. (As you know by now, I didn't always have the best experiences with the phone!) It was for me.

My dad and I had barely spoken in the last several months. He'd just seen my grades. His question still plays in my head: "How do you expect to get into college with grades like this?"

I didn't know. *How could an idiot like me get into college?* I stayed in my room, curled up on my bed, and cried the rest of the night.

Where was my hero? Where was my encourager? Where was my understanding shoulder? Where was the person who should have known that I was getting home close to nine o'clock at night several days a week because of school activities meant to gain some attention, but ultimately serving as an escape from the loneliness and worry that were eating me up inside?

It didn't seem fair. It didn't feel right. Something was wrong. And, once again, I would beat myself up and believe it was me. For me, it was much easier to believe that I was the one always to blame because then I wouldn't have to think about feeling like a pebble in my dad's shoe. I wouldn't have to question my dad's love.

It was the whole head-heart connection thing we talked about earlier. . . . I didn't have that. I wasn't too sure this dad who God gave me on earth harbored love in his heart for me. So, my heart couldn't quite understand that this same Father was a loving daddy. No, my heart could not seem to fully trust Him.

One day life happened. Life happened and it was ugly. I was on my face in tears surrendering my broken life to God. I'd been a believer for a long time and realized that I was holding on to everything too tightly. I wasn't trusting God with anything. So, I prayed and offered it all to God — my job, my mom's marriage, and the man I wanted to marry. Much to my dismay, He answered. He answered by taking it all. No kidding. He took me up on my offer.

I was clueless as to what would follow in the days ahead. My job was a wreck. I was miserable. The man God has convinced me will be my husband announces that he has never taken his old girlfriend "off the shelf." He goes on to tell me that he doesn't care for me at the same level he cared for her and that he's been having dreams with her in them. He wasn't so sure if God was trying to tell him that he needed to pursue her for a relationship. Ha. Good one, God. Needless to say, I was not a happy camper. We decided to call it quits and not speak for a while.

The next day at work I was holding it together pretty well when I heard the dreaded ringing of the phone. It was my mom. My step-dad sort

Daddy, Do You Love Me?

of left her. He wasn't too sure that he wanted to see her again. Alrighty! Life was going just peachy. The one man in my life who had taken an interest in me as a father figure was bailing. Oh, and did I mention that my dad and I weren't on speaking terms for the last four years, either? Yeah. I could see every silver lining in those black clouds forming a cyclone around me.

I surrendered all this stuff to God and He took it — literally. I decided to seek some wisdom and encouragement from a mentor. We went to lunch and, surprise, surprise, I was a river of mascara. I told her how my life was falling to pieces around me (which most people would have agreed with!). Did she offer me a tissue and a hug? Did she empathize and tell me she was so sorry for my ache? Nope. Do you know what she said to me? "I think you need to forgive your dad. I think you should call him and forgive him." *I'm sorry? Were we talking about my dad? Did I mention anything about needing one more thing on my plate full of crappiness?*

I was dumbfounded. What kind of encouragement was that? Didn't she know I was in the pit of despair? Geesh. But I couldn't get it out of my head. I forced it, but it wouldn't take a rest. I attributed it to guilt — false guilt.

The following days and nights were horrible. Especially the nights. I would lay in bed and sob myself to sleep. Two o'clock in the morning would come and I would beg God through my tears to comfort me. *Please, God. Be my father, my friend, the lover of my soul. Fill all the holes that are in my heart. I can't do this. I can't take it. There has already been so much hurt in my life . . . why do I have to go through this? I am tired of hurting. Please, God. Take away my pain. I am so lonely. Why did You lead me to believe that we would be married?*

I pored over my Bible. It was my only solace. Somehow, I had peace. God brought me to a place within himself that passes understanding and gave me His peace. Never before had I experienced peace in my heart. Chaos had always run rampant. If you had told me it would be possible in those moments to have peace, I wouldn't have believed you. And then I experienced it for myself.

Noooo, I wasn't functioning on all cylinders, but I wasn't reduced to a puddle on the floor, either. I was still dealing with my mom's marriage situation. I say dealing because I seemed to be the one who had a strong relationship with my step-father; ergo, I felt pressure to talk to him and make things better. Ha! My fear of confrontation and abandonment had

Ariel Allison and Shelby Rawson

a grip on me so tightly I could hardly move just thinking about it. Me? Talk to him in the middle of all this junk? Doubtful.

One day after work I was doing a very mundane thing — taking a bath. Naturally, I was talking on the phone. (Don't you have telephone conversations in the bathtub?) I was talking to my friend Amy about the things my mentor had said to me. She thought it was a good idea, too. In a matter of minutes, I was overcome by the feeling that I might really need to call my dad. Upon confessing this to Amy, she told me it sounded like God was trying to tell me something and I'd better do it.

It was the strangest feeling. I couldn't get out of the bathtub fast enough. My heart was pounding, but I knew what I had to do. I had to call him. I had to call the man I hadn't spoken to in over four years to tell him that I loved him, I wanted to move on, and I didn't want to live in the past. That was it. I had nothing else to say. No questions, and I wasn't in need of any answers. So, after nearly hyperventilating, I did it. I called.

He wasn't there. I left a message on his answering machine telling him exactly what God had put in my heart. Whew. I took a deep breath. I didn't cry. I just took a deep breath . . . of relief. For the first time, I wanted desperately for my dad to know I loved him. For the first time, I wasn't desperate for him to assure me of his love. Yes! Finally!! I loved him with no expectations. It was a gift that I had to give . . . that I wanted to give. I was no longer looking to receive love from him, but looking to give it. Never had the power of the Holy Spirit been more evident in my life.

That's not the end. He called me back within the hour and we had our first conversation in more than four long years. It wasn't the easiest or most natural interaction that I've ever had, but it was better than most of my interactions with anyone else. By the time we hung up the phone, a piece of me began to heal.

Within those minutes, God was moving milestones. You see, there were prayers that I'd never had the courage to utter. I had buried some of the greatest yearnings of my heart for fear that they would never be requited, but all my life, He knew. God knew what I so badly wanted to hear from the lips of my dad. That night, I heard them. That night, I became a little girl. My Daddy took me into His arms and showed me that He could meet my deepest needs and my buried yearnings without my ever mustering the courage to ask. He whispered into my ear and shouted

Daddy, Do You Love Me?

into my heart, "*I have called you by name; you are Mine*" *[Isa. 43:1;NAS95] Shelby Renee, you are Daddy's little girl. You are My little girl.*

That is how I believe in my head *and heart* that I am Daddy's little girl.

Endnotes

1. Madeline L'Engle, *Walking on Water: Reflections of Faith and Art* (Colorado Springs, CO: Shaw Books, 2001), p. 82–83.

2. Ibid.

3. http://www.infuzemag.com/narnia/archives/2005/11/hes_not_safe_bu.html

4. Wayne Kirkpatrick, sung by Michael W. Smith, "Never Been Unloved" (Reunion Records, 1998).

5. Kyle Pruett, *Fatherneed* (New York: The Free Press, 1999).

It Isn't Easy

Where the grace of God is missed, bitterness is born. But where the grace of God is embraced, forgiveness flourishes. The longer we walk in the garden, the more likely we are to smell like flowers. The more we immerse ourselves in grace, the more likely we are to give grace.

> — Max Lucado
> *In the Grip of Grace* [1]

> One who hates must dig two graves.
> — Old Proverb

She has no memories of living in the same house with him. Other men would come and go, but not him. Her first mental picture of him was at about age four. He was coming to see her sister. She remembers the car driving up the street, her sister loading up and the two of them driving away. She was supposed to be left behind. Tears welled up in her eyes as her naivete prevented any explanation from lending itself to her unguided heart. All her mind could grasp was that he came, he left, and Daddy didn't take her with him.

Her sister was off to have adventures with their dad, adventures that she would not be invited to take part in. She watched helplessly as their bond was being forged in front of her longing eyes. She recalls the delight in his eyes as he loaded the bags into his car and wondered why he didn't look at her with that expression.

She never did seem to get that same response from him. Joy was a face he saved for his other daughter. But this daughter . . . this daughter never stopped yearning for it. She wanted it. Somehow she must learn how to get it. How could she get joy instead of rejection? How could she get her dad to approve instead of frown on her?

Performance became her driving force. Fear became her fuel. Grade after grade, report card after report card. No response. No notice. So she would join in as her sister played sports with him. Yet, her own games did not hold the same weight as her sister's. They didn't seem as important. She would learn to force herself to stuff it, stuff the pain of rejection deep inside where no one could see it — including her. Still, she would perform. If nothing else, she would just be so good and do so well that he couldn't say anything bad, right?

But, she wasn't built like her sister. She didn't have long, skinny legs. There was no way that her body would ever don a slim size. A little girl in a 12 regular wasn't a stick, but she wasn't a marshmallow puff, either. In the middle of third grade, she would learn that her body wasn't okay, and neither were her teeth. Her dad would disgustedly let her know they were too yellow. He wanted her to brush with baking soda until they were clean. So she did.

Looking back, she finds herself a bit speechless. She wasn't the chosen daughter. She didn't have the right grades. She didn't have the right body. Heck, she didn't even have the right teeth. As she looks in the mirror today, she is disgusted by her body. The reflection of her legs can nearly bring tears to her eyes as she views them with nothing less than shame and abhorrence. At the same time, she practices her smile hoping to find one that won't appear quite so awful in pictures.

Daddy, Do You Love Me?

She is trapped by his words. Bound by his wounds. Silently, she comforts herself, *A little girl should never have felt that way. I didn't have the tools to work through those things on my own. You hurt me without hesitation. And your thoughtlessness crushed me. I deserved better. I tried so hard to please you. Why did my heart remain hidden from your affection? You should have noticed me. You should have seen me. I should never, ever have felt invisible."*

She felt gypped. She felt robbed. More than that, she was mad. And, God, where the heck was He in this whole mess? Why didn't He help matters? Why didn't He make her dad realize what he was doing? Her emotions ran high as her questions ran on. She had an intense desire to move on . . . move past it . . . get over it. Whatever it took, she just wanted to forget about the pain and be done with it. No more hard questions with seemingly harder answers. The pain was enough. She didn't want to feel it any more. And the realization that he could still hurt her without making a move just made her anger burn that much hotter.

As she grew older, she began meeting more and more people whose own fathers had passed away. They would encourage her to make amends with her dad before it was too late. *Don't they know that it's his turn to go out on a limb? It's his turn to take a step toward his invisible child.* They were clueless to the dues she'd paid. Her legs were tired of taking futile steps in his direction. *They weren't noticed as a kid, and they won't be noticed now.*

These were the same people who seemed to be shoving the word "forgiveness" down her throat. She had tried that and she didn't feel much different. He wasn't interested in her forgiveness. He'd never admitted that he'd done anything wrong. Besides, it wasn't as if she hated him. She just didn't want anything to do with him.

At the end of the day, she convinced herself they were better off like this. Who needs healing, anyway?

WHO IS DESERVING OF FORGIVENESS?

There are some nasty, nasty people in this world. There are Charles Mansons and Jeffrey Dahmers, serial killers and rapists. There are Timothy McVeys and Twin Tower crashers. Murderers. Nutjobs. Sickos. People who have absolutely no regard for human life. Their consciences are corrupt. Their brains are backwards. Remorse does not appear to enter their vocabulary. To think of the things these people have done causes a visceral response in my body. Some of their crimes are so gruesome that describing them would leave images in my brain for days, weeks, or longer. Who can forget the sight of men and women holding hands and plummeting to their death on September 11th? Who can forget the casualties of the Oklahoma City bombing? Who can ever forget the emotions that overwhelmed a country when its people were slain?

Scum. Filth. Twisted freaks. That is what you're thinking, isn't it? I'd be lying if I said those words never entered my mind. These jerks who stole human life don't deserve a better life, do they? They don't deserve my energy, much less my compassion or grace. Grace for killers? Grace for men who destroy? You've got to be kidding! I mean, aren't these people well beyond the point of deserving grace? Lock them up and throw away — no — incinerate the key!

Well, maybe these unfortunate souls are beyond human grace, but I am not so sure that matters in the end. We make decisions throughout life regarding the recipients of our own grace. Cross me once . . . here's a little grace. Cross me twice . . . not too sure you're worthy. We don't always feel up to the task of doling out second chances. Sometimes they just don't seem to be deserved. Sometimes a second chance just seems too dangerous . . . possibly a bit hurtful. In a way, *we* decide who we deem worthy of grace. People who cause others heart-wrenching grief, pain, and anguish are not generally thought of as deserving to be on the list.

We definitely don't picture ourselves in heaven standing at the throne of grace beside some wacko who committed murder, do we? No way! Their actions are outside the bell curve of God's favor, right?

Hold on just one little second. So now we're deciding who gets our grace and God's grace? Think about it. That is exactly what's happening. We have taken it upon ourselves to determine those people to whom the high King of heaven should bestow grace. Sounds dramatic, but it doesn't make it any less true.

JUST FOR ME — NOT YOU

Did you know that the murdering cannibal Jeffrey Dahmer expressed remorse and repented of his crimes? Yep. You heard me. That psycho became a follower of Christ and was even baptized to show his belief publicly. He was forgiven. Let me rephrase, he *is* forgiven. Do you know what else? He'll be standing right next to us at the throne of grace! Not on a lower step designated for those less worthy, but right up there with you and me.

 Daddy, Do You Love Me?

It doesn't rest easy with me that a horrific murderer gets the same grace that I do. It doesn't seem fair. Shouldn't fingers be pointed at him instead of welcoming him? In our heart of hearts, we really want to be his judge and jury. Who are *we* to feel this way?

> Who is this person? It could be anyone ("O man, whoever you are") who filters God's grace through his own opinion. Anyone who dilutes God's mercy with his own prejudice. He is the prodigal son's elder brother who wouldn't attend the party (see Luke 15:11–32). He is the ten-hour worker, upset because the one-hour worker got the same wage (see Matt. 20:1–16). He is the fault-finding brother obsessed by his brother's sins and oblivious to his own (Max Lucado).[2]

Who is this person? It's me. It's you. We are guilty of withholding grace. Don't believe me? Then try to picture this: God running out to embrace one of His reckless sons — your dad. Can you picture it? The same Daddy who runs to protect and hold His daughter would also be willing to run to the man who wounded her to the core? What? What?!! B-b-but he doesn't deserve it!

My dad hasn't earned the right to be accepted into the gracious hands of my Father. He hasn't atoned for what he's done to me. He hasn't paid for it.

Like I said, we want to be judge and jury — especially for our dads. Guess what? No dice. Not gonna happen. God is the only true judge. There is no jury. We don't get a vote. According to God, "There is no-one who does good, not even one" (Rom. 3:12; NIV). Not your dad, not me, not Mother Teresa, and not you. Not one of us is deserving of the grace of God.

There is only one way that any of us are allowed the grace of the Father and that is through His Son Jesus Christ. "It is through Christ that all of us are able to come into the presence of the Father" (Eph. 2:18; TEV).

Max Lucado's book, *In The Grip of Grace*, tells a story of yet another murderer.

> Each week Kevin Tunell is required to mail a dollar to a family he'd rather forget. They sued him for $1.5 million but settled for $936, to be paid a dollar at a time. The family expects the payment each Friday so Tunell won't forget what happened on the first Friday of 1982.

Ariel Allison and Shelby Rawson

That's the day their daughter was killed. Tunell was convicted of manslaughter and drunken driving. He was 17. She was 18. Tunell served a court sentence. He also spent seven years campaigning against drunk driving, six years more than his sentence required. But he keeps forgetting to send the dollar.

The weekly restitution is to last until the year 2000. Eighteen years. Tunell makes the check out to the victim, mails it to her family, and the money is deposited in a scholarship fund.

The family has taken him to court four times for failure to comply. After the most recent appearance, Tunell spent 30 days in jail. He insists that he's not defying the order but rather is haunted by the girl's death and tormented by the reminders. He offered the family two boxes of checks covering the payments until the year 2001, one year more than required. They refused. It's not money they seek, but penance.

Quoting the mother, "We want to receive the check every week on time. He must understand we are going to pursue this until August of the year 2000. We will go back to court every month if we have to."[3]

Few would question the anger of the family. Only the naïve would think it fair to leave the guilty unpunished. But I do have one concern. Are 936 payments enough? Not for Tunell to send, mind you, but for the family to demand? When they receive the final payment, will they be at peace? In August 2000, will the family be able to put the matter to rest? Is 18 years of restitution sufficient? Will 196 months worth of remorse be adequate?

How much is enough? Were you in the family and were Tunnel your target, how many payments would you require? Better stated, how many payments do you require?[4]

A LITTLE PAIN, PLEASE

So, how many is it? If your dad could pay you for your pain, how much would it take? How long do you think his payments should be due to make him understand the devastation he caused in your heart? Maybe you don't want money. You just want suffering or humiliation. Yeah, humiliation would be great. Let him be the one whose eyes become flooded with tears when witnessing a tender moment between a father and daughter. Oooh! What about a little emotional turmoil and heinous flashbacks for the rest of his life? Now we're talking.

I think Faith Hill puts the tune to these thoughts rather well:

> Could you cry a little?
> Die just a little?
> Pretend that you're feeling a little more pain?
> Again, all I'm wanting is something in return.
> Could you cry a little for me?[5]

Yeah, buddy. That would make it better, wouldn't it? Your pain would let up if your dad was knocked down a smidgen. Sure it would. That's how it always works. . . . Give them a taste of their own medicine and you will find healing.

Do you really believe that? Search your heart. You know it's not true. You may want it to be true, but that won't make it so. Pay close attention to this. Your dad cannot make up for the pain he's caused you. He cannot do it. He has no divine powers. No healing balm to place on your heart. And hating him won't improve your condition, either. The reality is this: "[Your father's debt is] far greater than his power to repay."[6]

He can never EVER make up for your pain. This man who is responsible for so much of the agony of your life is not capable of settling up on the debt he owes. Your dad cannot pay you back, nor can he pay God back. Did you catch that? You are not the only one to whom your father is indebted. Ultimately, he owes the Father far more than he owes his daughter, *and you owe the Father far more than your father owes you.*

Zinger! I know. I know. I'm sort of sticking it to you, but I am not telling you anything that I don't know to be true. Sure, your dad may have been, or may be, the scum of the earth. Unfortunately, he isn't the standard — Jesus Christ is. He is the only completely perfect being to ever grace the face of the earth. Yes, this is the same Christ who loves His daughters when they are sleazy, dopey, grumpy, and stupid.

Who is this perfect Christ person, anyway? He, my friends, is the only Son of God who endured slander, beatings beyond recognition, and spikes driven through His flesh while hanging on a cross to keep us from being separated from the love of a Holy God. God wants us to live without sin. We can't manage to do it. For this reason, Jesus steps in and goes to bat for those who believe in Him. He took punishment for us when He'd done nothing wrong. He did nothing to deserve the pain which He endured. This pain is what we cause Him when we lie, sleep around, punish unmercifully, and withhold grace and forgiveness from someone. We owe Jesus Christ something we cannot possibly repay — *life*.

Why shouldn't you withhold grace? Why should you give grace where it doesn't seem to be deserved? Because you have been given grace beyond merit by a perfect Son. Those that walk with Him also walk in His forgiveness. *Forgiveness*. The price has already been paid for your daddy's sin. Not by him. Not by you. By Him "whose sandals [we are] not fit to carry" (Matt. 3:11; NIV).

No matter how much it stings, we are called by God to forgive just as we have been forgiven. Frankly, forgiving stinks some of the time. It's not fun. There are times when it requires dealing with some pretty horrible memories. Quite often, mustering up the strength to forgive feels more like torture. I can promise you this: it feels nothing like gasping for breath while nailed to a tree.

IT'S UP TO YOU

So here's my question. Have you done it? What I mean is, have you forgiven the man that gave you life yet? Notice I didn't say the man who made your life great, happy, or safe. He did give you something — life. Are you ready to forgive? Maybe you're still suffocating in your anger or hurt . . . choking on choices he made. Desperately hoping he will come to the realization that he screwed up — and you got stuck paying the emotional check. You may very well be completely accurate in your assessment. Sooo, how's that workin' for ya?

It would make things so much nicer if he would grovel a little and beg for your forgiveness, huh? That way you can feel a little superior and have pity on the poor man. You can work out a dramatic, theatrical scene in your head of how it will play out:

You are at a public place. (The mall might be good.) Today is your birthday and you are surrounded by close friends. They all know the heartache you have endured because of your relationship with your father. Suddenly, you are approached by a man looking forlorn and desperate.

"Sweetie!" says the man.

"Yes. I'm sorry. Do I know you?" you reply.

"It's me, princess, your wretched, awful father."

Daddy, Do You Love Me?

(Your friends gasp in disbelief and shock as they bear witness to the occasion.)

"What —?" you say.

"Please, please don't say another word," interjects your lowly father. "Let me speak. I know that I have made your life miserable. You should have been hugged and affirmed. I should have told you that you were pretty and talented. I should have come to all of your activities. I should have let you paint my fingernails. I wish I had never said a cross word to you." Through sobs, he continues. "What can I do to repay you? What must I do to earn your forgiveness, my dear, sweet, darling daughter?"

Wouldn't this make it easier on you? He grovels and you get to choose to grant his wish. Yeah, that sounds just like true forgiveness. It practically screams grace, don't you think? Uh-huh . . . sure . . . and maybe pigs will fly out of the ice, too.

> Forgiveness is the soil in which God nurtures our emotional healing and our ability to love once again.[7]
> — John Nieder and Thomas M. Thompson,
> *Forgive & Love Again*

Keeping your wounds bound to your belt can be a bit burdensome, don't you think? No one can force you to take the belt off. You need to make a choice. You must choose to throw it off and get rid of it. Don't put it somewhere to be picked up and worn again. It's time to let go and free yourself from the weight of woundedness. It doesn't mean that your memories are going to magically disappear or be abducted by aliens. You will probably still shed some tears as you struggle. However, it will allow you to move forward in your life and forgive an imperfect man. No relationship will ever fully develop until you can make this decision.

Forgiving your dad starts with you. *You* need to make a choice to forgive him in the absence of his asking for it. Why? Because he may never ask, he may never seek it, and he may not want it. True forgiveness is not coupled with reconciliation. It is not based on the response of someone else. It is found within the heart of the offended.

Forgiving your dad is not about his life, *it's about yours*. The power to let go of the past is in your hands. The power to shed the dead weight of bitterness, anger, and hate rests solely with you. Take off your millstone.

A friend of mine penned the words to this song:

Ariel Allison and Shelby Rawson

He's kinda mellowed in his old age, but the memories remain.
She keeps bearing all the burdens, as if to keep alive the pain.
She can't erase the scars she's got from every word and every blow,
But she's finding part of growing up is learning to let go.
Down the long road to forgiveness there is fear at every turn
And she knows she needs to go the distance,
Where her heart can finally rest,
Break these chains of bitterness,
Down the long road to forgiveness.
She's pointed fingers and stood her ground
And built a wall around her heart.
She didn't want to lose a battle in a war she did not start.
She's carried grudges long enough
And they've only weighed her down,
Now the bridges burned are just lessons learned
that she carries with her now.
Down the long road to forgiveness
There is fear at every turn,
And she knows she needs to go the distance
Where her heart can finally rest,
Break these chains of bitterness,
Down the long road to forgiveness.[8]

Let your heart take a rest. Break free of your bitter chains. Forgive the unforgivable. Forgive your dad.

UNFORGIVENESS IS BAD FOR YOUR HEALTH

The memory comes unbidden, triggered by something simple: a picture, a movie, a song on the radio. Your dad is in your head once again. Perhaps it was something he said when you were five, or maybe it was only five days ago. Something he did or didn't do. Your jaw clenches. It is more than emotional, it is a physical reaction that grips your body. Tears well up at the corners of your eyes. You purse your lips or maybe grind your teeth. You *feel* it, and you hold that emotion not only in your heart, but in your body as well. This isn't the first time that memory has assailed you, and it isn't the first time that your body has tensed in reaction to it. It happens over and over, countless times, in different memories.

What you may not realize is that the unforgiveness you harbor in your heart is very bad for your physical health. God has known it all along, but only in the last few years has science begun to understand the devastation that harboring grudges has, not only on our emotional health, but our physical health, as well.

Take the findings in this recent article for example:

TUESDAY, March 27 *(HealthScout)* — To forgive is divine — and apparently healthy, too.

Nursing grudges and reminding yourself of events that caused you pain, on the other hand, can damage your health, claims a new study. Just briefly imagining a painful event and rehearsing your feelings can raise your blood pressure and heart rate, the researchers say.

"When people focused on unforgiving thoughts, often they felt more physical stress and more negative emotions," says lead author Charlotte vanOyen Witvliet, a psychology professor at Hope College in Holland, Michigan.

Forgiveness, however, offers an unexpected gift: more positive emotions and decreases in stress levels, Witvliet says.

"In doing this merciful gift-giving, we're often the recipients of the greatest benefits," she says. And in the long run, Witvliet says, chronic unforgiveness could wreak havoc on a person's health.

"These were real physical effects associated with just thinking about a person," she says. Imagine, she says, relationships that include banged doors and heated arguments — over dozens of years. "The accumulated effects over time that are going to chip away at very physical systems will have an effect on various health issues" she says.

For the study, the researchers asked 71 college students to recall a situation in which someone hurt them. They then assessed how their bodies reacted as the participants spent two hours seesawing between imagery sessions involving unforgiveness and forgiveness. Each session lasted about 16 seconds and ended with a relaxation period.

During the unforgiveness sessions, the participants rehearsed the hurt they'd experienced, meaning they replayed the events

Ariel Allison and Shelby Rawson

and their feelings like a movie. They also practiced harboring a grudge, Witvliet says. The script, she says, read, "Think about how unfair it was for this person to hurt you and how you'd like them to feel bad about it."

The students' heart rates rose from a baseline of 1.75 beats every four seconds to nearly three beats during the rehearsal sessions, the study says, and to 2.6 when they harbored grudges. Similarly, blood pressure rose 2.5 mm/Hg in a four-second period when the students either rehearsed the hurtful experience or harbored grudges.

By contrast, focusing on the offender's human qualities — gaining empathy for him or her — prompted a participant's heart rate to drop an average of a half-beat every four seconds, the study says. And imagining actively forgiving, including relinquishing a desire for vengeance and moving to wanting good fortune for the offender, also brought a small drop in the heart rate. Findings appear in the March 2001 issue of *Psychological Science*.

Everett Worthington, head of the psychology department at Virginia Commonwealth University and executive director of the nonprofit Campaign for Forgiveness Research, says research into forgiveness is producing a lot of hard evidence that dovetails with Witvliet's findings.

For instance, Worthington says, his own research shows that people in happy marriages have much lower levels of cortisol than those in unhappy marriages. Cortisol is a hormone activated by stress, and higher levels of cortisol would produce the kind of heart rate and blood pressure changes Witvliet found, he says.

If you're unforgiving, you're in a constant state of desiring change, and that's stressful, Worthington says. Unforgiveness also includes resentment, bitterness, hostility, hatred, anger, and fear — all of which are stressful, he says.

Life-threatening problems occur, he says, not when you won't forgive a single person, but when you're unforgiving in all your relationships.

"It's going to increase your risk factors for cardiovascular problems and stress-related disorders," Worthington says. "There's the type-A hostility that causes those cardiovascular problems."

Daddy, Do You Love Me?

Sometimes people associate forgiveness with weakness, Witvliet says, thinking it means yielding control over their lives to the person who hurt them. But ironically, she says, participants in the study reported that forgiving gave them more positive thoughts and also a stronger sense of control over their lives.

"Forgiveness is not about excuses or tolerating or condoning or letting the person off the hook," Witvliet says. Sometimes it includes actually breaking off a relationship with a person if that person continues to be hurtful, she adds.

"But that doesn't mean in our hearts we can't let go of bitterness and hurt and try to cultivate positive thoughts and feelings toward that person," Witvliet says.[9]

By Julia McNamee Neenan

Dr. G.A. Pettitt, (MA, MSE (Psych), MRCP, FRNZCGP, DObstRCOG) of Whole Life Endeavours in Nelson, New Zealand, has this to say about the effects of unforgiveness on the human body:

The fact is that after you have been hurt, humiliated, angry, suffered fear or loss, real or false guilt, or envy, etc., the unforgiveness, the blocked flow of love, profoundly affects the way your body functions, and thus your health. This is mediated by alterations in the patterns of chemicals and electricity in your body.

For example, your muscles may tighten, causing imbalances or pain in your neck, back, and limbs. Headaches may occur. There is decreased blood flow to the joint surfaces. This makes it more difficult for the blood to remove wastes from the tissues. It reduces the supply of oxygen and nutrients to the cells. This increases the likelihood of delayed or inadequate repair during sleep, impairing recovery from injury, arthritis, etc. Your teeth clench at night contributing to problems with your teeth and jaw joints. Injury through inattention, accident, or violence is more likely. The peptide and hormonal chemical "messengers" are altered in every system of the body.

The blood flow to your heart is constricted. Your digestion is impaired. Your breathing is restricted. Your immune system functions less well, and you become more vulnerable to infections, and perhaps malignancy. You feel bad, and your mind is less able to see its way through problems and difficulties. The list could go on. Indeed, it becomes a list of many of the diseases seen by doctors all over the world. And while unforgiveness may not be the sole cause of all of them, it increases your vulnerability to them. It can "set the scene" for them, and it can delay, or even prevent, your recovery.[10]

That should make you think twice about that "little" grudge you're holding. It isn't such a small thing after all. For some of us, it's much more than a grudge, it is pure, raw hate, and we know it, but now we know that it is literally killing us, as well. How ironic to think that the one we are trying to hurt by not letting go is getting away scot-free. Your unforgiveness is more than likely not hurting dad at all — unless he has asked for it and you are purposefully withholding it out of spite. In that case, he's got hurt feelings but nothing more. You, on the other hand, are rotting inside. Dying, literally.

Now that we understand how science has caught up to Scripture, let's go back to God and see what He has to say on the subject:

> But love your enemies, and do good, and lend, expecting nothing in return; and your reward will be great, and you will be sons of the Most High; for He Himself is kind to ungrateful and evil men. Be merciful, just as your Father is merciful (Luke 6:35–36; NAS95).

God himself is kind to ungrateful and evil men.

Ungrateful and evil. Your dad may never ask for your forgiveness and he may not want it. That is utterly beside the point. You have been commanded to give it. God doesn't require it of us because He is the big cosmic killjoy, but because unforgiveness is destroying His daughter. Remember friend, whose daughter you really are.

> When we see our enemies from God's perspective, compassion follows, for He has seen the sorrows in their hearts that have caused them to behave in such a manner. He longs to reach out to these people and comfort them, and He sometimes uses our hands to do it.[11]

— Elaine Wright Colvin and Elaine Creaseman
Treasury of God's Virtues

Daddy, Do You Love Me?

THE BATTLE TO LET GO

Forgiveness isn't easy. It isn't supposed to be. If it were, it would require no faith and then it would be about us instead of God. Sometimes forgiveness does not come in an instant. We make the choice to forgive in a single moment, but the letting go often takes a great deal of time as we continually return to the One who has forgiven *us* and release the anger we are harboring.

But you want to move on — to forgive. Perhaps you ponder the idea that many of us are not always worthy of someone's forgiveness. That's where grace and mercy come into play. Do you have it in you to extend it to your father? Can you choose to grow past this place that has chained itself around your neck like an anchor?

A healing prayer from Jon Eargle, *Healing Where You Hurt . . . On the Inside:*

> *Father, we praise You for Your healing mercy. Thank You for loving and accepting us with all our hurts, hang-ups, and sins, but thank You even more for caring enough to change us. Thank You for saving us from ourselves and our unwittingly self-destructive tendencies. We reach out and open up to receive Your tender mercies, praising You for showing us that we are forgiven so that we may be able to forgive — both ourselves and others! Amen.*[12]

Shelby's Thoughts

This is a tough one. The title of the chapter is no joke. It isn't easy to forgive your dad. And, surprisingly, friends don't always encourage you to do it! Sometimes they make it worse by telling you that you don't need to! They obviously don't understand what hanging on to that kind of junk does to a person. Any who. . . . It took me several years to do it. I tried over and over to let go of the hurt and bitterness. Several times I was convinced that I had done it. After all, I'd prayed about it and said the words to God more than once. In my mind, that should have taken care of it.

Still, the thought of seeing him brought a rise of anxiousness to my stomach. The idea of hearing his voice on the phone produced a sense of uneasiness that could stop me in my tracks. I was beginning to realize that one of the things that accompanies forgiveness is peace.

Ariel Allison and Shelby Rawson

In chapter 5 I told you about a phone call I'd made to my dad. That was the first time in four years that I felt a peace about speaking to him. It was the only time in my life that I had finally let everything go. I wasn't able to forgive my dad on my own. I needed God's help. Boy, oh boy, did He show up and meet me in my need. Forgiveness of my dad was about God's timing — not my own. No matter how much I had pressured my heart to move on, it just wouldn't. At least, it wouldn't until the time was right.

At long last, I was completely ready to forgive my dad. Before I dialed the numbers, my heart called on God. He took those burdens that night before a word was uttered between the two of us. I had no idea what to expect from my him, but one thing I was sure of: I did not need to hear my father say he was sorry in order to offer forgiveness. My forgiveness was already secured — whether he wanted it, or not.

So he returned my call. We shot the breeze for a little bit and then the conversation turned. My dad apologized. Not only did I get to hear him say he was sorry, but I was able to hear something else, too. "I hope you can forgive me." Wow. I had never imagined him saying that to me. The amazing thing was that I responded in all honesty that I already had. I was overwhelmingly blessed. I had experienced forgiveness that night like no other time in my life.

The most amazing thing that God showed me through all the stuff with my dad was that every woman has a little princess inside them, standing in her best dress and waiting for her daddy to dazzle her heart and make it dance. While she waits — unbeknownst to her — there is a God who is rejoicing over her with singing. God showed me that the only perfect Father I would ever know is Him. In one night, He took my heart tenderly in the strength of His love and my heart finally heard His song. A song He sings only to me. He chose to reveal this to me at the same time that my dad and I made steps toward reconciliation. And my heart was free to love my dad as he is — a fallen man — instead of desperately hoping to love him as my hero.

Ariel's Thoughts

I won't soon forget the day that I took my first step on the long road to forgiving my father. It was a long road indeed.

I was 20 years old and working at my first real job. It was ten o'clock in the morning and I was so angry I wanted to throw my computer

Daddy, Do You Love Me?

through an office window. Moments earlier I had learned that my father was in town, and had been in town for three months without so much as a phone call. To make matters worse, this was the second time in the last year that he'd pulled that little stunt. He'd come to work with and visit my older brother, and I wasn't even worth a phone call. The longer I stewed over it, the angrier I became. I wasn't the beloved first-born son, I was the ignored second-born daughter, had always been, would always be. I was irate. I was heartbroken. The truth of the matter was that I felt totally rejected.

So I called a friend, looking for sympathy. I wanted someone to be angry with me and tell me that I had a right to hate him. No such luck.

"Ariel, have you forgiven your father?"

I was stunned. "*What?*"

My sweet friend Terri Howard rephrased the question because my response had been an obvious "No!"

"Ariel, are you willing to be *willing* to forgive your father?"

She knew that right then I was not willing, but she wanted me to consider being willing to forgive him.

I began crying hysterically, overcome with emotions that I couldn't describe. I didn't answer her that day and the only other thing I remember about our conversation is that she prayed for me.

I thought about her words a lot, and I could not escape the truth of them. I needed to forgive my father. I wish I could say that in a moment of surrender and total humility I released my anger, bitterness, hate, and disappointment. The truth of the matter is that it simply did not happen that way for me. I struggled deeply and I struggled daily. Sometimes it felt as though I had to surrender each offense individually. I can't count the times that I forgave him and then found myself hating him once again for the very thing that I thought I had surrendered to God. For me, forgiveness did not happen overnight, it was a process and it took *years*.

I was a bit like the pendulum on a clock, swinging back and forth in my responses toward my father: grace and resentment, grace and resentment, grace and resentment. Then the severe mercy of God caught up with me three years later when my father was diagnosed with terminal cancer. I was forced into a time frame not of my own choosing. I had been leisurely offering grace, on my terms, but God wanted me to surrender it all. No more picking and choosing.

Ariel Allison and Shelly Rawson

I have come to believe that God allowed me to struggle with forgiveness so I would be forced to run back to the Cross. Forced to remember the debt that I owe to God. Forced to remember that I too am a broken creature in need of forgiveness. It was during his struggle with cancer that something inside of me finally broke. I could not look at his frail body and hold my hate any longer. I found myself praying for more time with him, praying that God would extend his life.

It was during that long summer that I remembered a bout with cancer my father had endured when I was in my early teens. I hated him so badly during that period of my life that I actually prayed he would die. It is amazing how forgiveness changes our hearts. During his second battle with cancer, the one that finally claimed his life, I prayed that he would be healed.

Somewhere in the mix, I found that I had truly and finally forgiven him, and it was ultimate freedom. It wasn't something I was trying to withhold from him, merely something I didn't know how to really let go. Mentally, I had acknowledged him forgiven, but emotionally there were things I was clinging to, pains that I liked to brood over. One by one, they had to be ripped from my heart.

Am I still a wounded little girl that desperately needs a daddy? Yes, and I always will be. That is okay, because the Daddy I have will never die. He is eternal and He is perfect, and in the moments where I surrender my heart, He wraps His arms around me and cradles me like the child I am. And I am learning to let Him.

Endnotes

1. Max Lucado, *In the Grip of Grace* (Dallas, TX: Word Publishing, 1996).

2. Ibid., p. 37.

3. Ibid, p. 149–150.

4. Ibid., p. 153.

5. Angie Aparo, "Cry" sung by Faith Hill (Warner Records, 2002).

6. Lucado, *In the Grip of Grace*.

7. John Nieder and Thomas M. Thompson, *Forgive & Love Again* (Eugene, OR: Harvest House Publishers, 1991).

Daddy, Do You Love Me?

8. Words and music by David James White and Joanna Janet, Everytown Music Publications, Inc., ©2003.

9. http://wcautvhealth.ip2m.com/index.cfm?pt=itemDetail&item_id=10569&site_cat_id=8

10. http://www.iloveulove.com/downloads/Forgiveness%20&%20Health%201999.pdf

11. Elaine Wright Colvin and ElaineCreaseman, *Treasury of God's Virtues* (Lincolnwood, IL: Publications International, 1999).

12. Jon Eargle, *Healing Where You Hurt . . . On the Inside* (Jon Eargle Ministries, 1981).

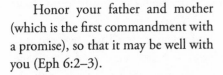

Honor your father and mother (which is the first commandment with a promise), so that it may be well with you (Eph 6:2–3).

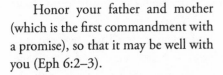

Chapter 7

We are all pencils in the hand of a writing God, who is sending love letters to the world.

— Mother Teresa

Words — so innocent and powerless as they are, as standing in a dictionary, how potent for good and evil they become in the hands of one who knows how to combine them.

— Nathaniel Hawthorne

I don't know why he picked today, of all days, to show up," she mumbled loudly to anyone within earshot. "I guess my college graduation party is prestigious enough for him to attend. So very glad to see he has such high standards for himself. I'd hate for him to have sunk so low as to make an appearance for Christmas."

She made no attempt to disguise the disdain on her face as she watched him. *This is my day. Mine. You get absolutely no credit for it. Today has nothing to do with you and everything to do with me. Just try to take an itty bit of credit for it . . . we'll see how your newly found trophy daughter responds.*

His eyes were cast every which way but hers as he made his way across the room. He looked so uncomfortable, it was as if his skin wanted to escape the body it was bound to.

Good. You should be uncomfortable. What on earth made you come, anyway? You haven't made attempts to be involved in my life since the fifth grade. And then, you pretty much dropped off the face of the earth. Not even one response to my letters or cards. Not one! You jerk.

At this point, she had become pretty much oblivious to the people around her. Their conversations were like white noise. In the midst of the crowd her eyes were fixed on him. Before she knew it, there he was. Her dad was closer to her than he'd been in years. The tension was more than a knife could cut through.

"Hi."

"Hey."

Her friends tried to smile at this man they'd only heard about, but never met.

"A lot of people showed up for your party. That's really nice."

"Yeah. I've known a lot of these people for several years." She continued with condescension and sarcasm. "Some of them even watched my tennis matches in high school. And there are a few who actually gave me birthday cards and called me on holidays. Not that you would know anything about that now, would you? That's just not something that you had time for, huh? Oh, I know. It's very hard to find five minutes to dial the phone to speak with your daughter."

"Hon —"

"Honey?!! Don't call me honey! You haven't bothered to say my name in years, so don't attempt to use a word that might mean I'm actually special to you. We both know that's a joke! Just go. Live your life without me. That seems to be easier for you."

Without skipping a beat, she turned back to her friends who'd been watching in silence. "I can't believe he had the nerve to show up. I knew he was clueless, but I didn't know he was an idiot."

Daddy, Do You Love Me?

UNDERSTANDING HONOR

I'm going to be blatantly honest and admit that I have never really liked the fifth commandment. The others made sense to me. That one, however, always bothered me. I spent a lot of years pretending that there were only nine. Not only did I not *want* to honor my father, I simply didn't know how.

Before we go much further, I suppose it would prove well to define what "honoring" your father really looks like. It's probably best to get to the point right here before you get so discouraged or overwhelmed that you close the book. Because, you know what? I know what you're thinking. *"My dad doesn't deserve to be honored."* You are probably right, but that has nothing to do with the fact that God still requires you to honor him. It isn't optional. As a matter of fact, it is so important that it is one of the "Big Ten." You are *commanded* to honor your father. You are not given a choice. You *have* to do it. It is a sin not to.

Yet I have a feeling that what God has in mind is far different from what you think He is expecting of you. So for the next few pages I am going to draw wisdom from a man who has helped me clearly see what it means to honor my father. Dennis Rainey has given permission to use a series of devotions on this subject from his book, *Moments Together for Couples*.

> Honor, according to Webster's dictionary, is "a good name or public esteem. A showing of unusual merited respect." When God commands us to "Honor your father and your mother," however, He provides some additional meaning. In the original Hebrew language, the word for "honor" meant "heavy or weight." To honor someone meant "I weigh you down with respect and prestige. I place upon you great worth and value."
>
> It is fascinating to observe, as God originally formed Israel into a nation, that the concept of honoring parents was one of its foundational elements. Think of the setting: God had brought this nation of people, held captive for so long in Egypt, into the wilderness of Sinai. He had promised them the land of Israel, but up to this point He had never given them any written directions. They needed instructions to govern their behavior and preserve their identity as a nation.
>
> God gave them the Ten Commandments. So you can best appreciate the significance of the command to honor parents,

Ariel Allison and Shelby Rawson

note that the first four commandments dealt with how man relates to God. With these mandates, God established that He is the One who should be exalted above anyone or anything else. A nation's life, and an individual's life, is defined by its relationship with God.

Then comes the fifth commandment, and I don't think that's by coincidence. *Honoring parents should be a direct result of our faith in God* (italics mine).

Look carefully at the commandment again. Whom did God command us to honor? Only perfect parents? Only Christian parents? Parents who are spiritually mature and insightful? Only parents who never made major mistakes in rearing us? No, God commands us to honor our parents regardless of their performances, behaviors, and dysfunctions. Why? Because honoring parents demands that we walk by faith. . . .

Honoring your parents is a command for children of all ages. There is no exception clause in this command that exempts the adult child from responsibility. I can almost sense you starting to squirm in your seat. Honoring your parents seems risky.

Let me take a few moments to tell you what honoring your parents is, and what it isn't.

Honoring your parents does not mean endorsing irresponsibility or sin. It is not a denial of what they have done wrong as parents. It does not mean you flatter them by "emotionally stuffing" the mistakes they've made or denying the emotional or even the physical pain they may have caused you.

For an adult child, honoring your parents will not place you back under their authority. It does not give them access to manipulate you. It doesn't mean crawling back into the cradle and becoming a helpless child again.

Honoring your parents means choosing to place great value on your relationship with them.

Honoring your parents means taking the initiative to improve the relationship.

Honoring your parents means obeying them until you establish yourself as an adult.

Honoring your parents means recognizing what they've done right in your life.

Daddy, Do You Love Me?

Honoring your parents means recognizing the sacrifices they have made for you.

Honoring your parents means praising them for the legacy they are passing on to you.

Honoring your parents means seeing them through the eyes of Christ, with understanding and compassion.

Honoring your parents means forgiving them as Christ has forgiven you.

It is an attitude accompanied by actions that say to your parents, "You are worthy. You have value. You are the person God sovereignly placed in my life. . . ."

None of the other Ten Commandments has a promise attached to it. But how will it "be well with you" when you honor your parents?

I believe one profound reason is that it helps you finish the process of growing into adulthood. A part of maturing as an adult is the growing realization and conviction that you now share with your parents the responsibility for the relationship.[1]

I don't know about you, but after reading that, I feel a weight lift from my shoulders. Honoring my father doesn't mean I have to pretend he was anything different than he was. It means that I am obedient to God. It means that I have the opportunity to grow my character. There is most certainly reward in it for me.

THE NUTS AND BOLTS OF "HONOR"

So let's take a moment and talk about what that means practically. How can you honor your father in your daily life? For starters, I believe it means that you need to really start thinking about how you speak of your dad. Are your words filled with anger and spite every time you mention him? Do you take every opportunity you have to tear him down? There is a difference between acknowledging that you and your father are in the midst of a very difficult relationship and being a "dad-basher." Take the following statements for example.

You could say, "My dad is a real jerk (or alternate four-letter word). He is so stupid. You would think a grown man would know better, but not my dad. No, he's just a moron."

True perhaps, but not falling in the "honoring" category.

Ariel Allison and Shelby Rawson

Or you could say this: "You know, my father and I have had a really rough relationship. There are a lot of things he has done that have hurt me and disappointed me."

Both statements are honest and both describe the current state of that relationship. However, the latter still holds him in a place of honor. It does not pretend that he has been a good dad. It does acknowledge his place in your life.

This is important why, you ask? Because there are people listening to you talk about him. Perhaps it is younger family members or friends who will be tainted by your words and your attitudes. You have no business teaching other people how to hate your father. Nor do you have any right to shred his character in the presence of others. If you indulge in that, it puts you on the same level as the man who hurt you.

Don't get me wrong, there is a balance. Neither should you puff him up in front of others and make him out to be something he is not. Learning what to say and what not to say takes time. Sometimes it means shutting your mouth and not saying anything if you don't have something nice to say. (Hmm, maybe Mom was right about that!) Try practicing that for a while until you can learn the balance between honesty and honor. The next time you want to bash your dad, try saying something nice about him instead.

Lest you get the wrong idea about me, let me assure you that it has taken me many years to find that balance and I still say things that I regret on occasion. As a matter of fact, I have been called to account for my lack of honor by both my friends and my husband. Yeah, my dishonor has been blatant at times, and I was wrong to do it.

So what else does honoring my father mean? It means praying for him. It means being consistent about bringing him before Christ while you are on your knees. It is okay to ask God to change him, and it is appropriate to ask God to change you as well. Pray for his faults. Pray for your relationship. Thank God for everything you can think of about him. Thank God for progress if you're making any, and most certainly thank God for everything your father has done right in your life. Honor your father by bringing him before the One that ordained him as your dad.

Honor is a decision we make to place high value, worth, and importance on another person by viewing him or her as

Daddy, Do You Love Me?

a priceless gift and granting him or her a position in our lives worthy of great respect; and love involves putting that decision into action.[2]

— Gary Smalley and John Trent
The Gift of Honor

My guess is that you still love your dad. I'm sure there are other emotions in there, but for the vast majority of us, we still love him. I know I do. When was the last time that you told him? Whether or not he says it back doesn't matter. Try telling him the next time you talk to him. Say it every time you talk to him.

THE TRIBUTE

Honor. It really does evoke a sense of pride when you think of a person with honor. It brings to mind great heroes and humanitarians. A great example of someone with honor is the true story of Carl Brashear, who was played by Cuba Gooding Jr. in the movie *Men of Honor*. He put up with a mountain of ridicule and maltreatment because he wanted to be more than a black man swabbing the deck of a ship and working in the mess hall. Carl Brashear wanted to be the first African-American navy diver. No matter how horrid he was treated, he was not to be deterred, and although his trainer was determined to make him fail, he achieved his goal. Even after becoming a double-amputee (both lower legs) he battled in court to continue his diving.

This is the kind of man you want to stand up and cheer for! How amazing is it that he overcame such obstacles? When you watch his story unfold, you are bursting with pride that such a man has lived. The movie title makes perfect sense to you. Carl Brashear was honor personified. Every bit of respect and admiration was due him. He deserved to have tribute paid to his life, and so it was.

Yep, that is definitely the kind of life that deserves to be honored. At least, it's a life that seems *easy* to honor. It isn't too difficult to muster up distinction for a man like Brashear who overcame the odds. Still, I'm wondering . . . would you find it easy to admire him if he was a screwup as a dad? Let's pretend the movie was about your dad's success in the navy. Would you still agree with the title? Probably not. After all, you would know the true story behind the film. You would know that your dad messed up in a big way with his daughter. So, even if he was a navy hero, he wouldn't deserve one ounce of honor, right?

Axel Allison and Shelby Rawson

Honor is something we bestow upon great people, isn't it? Hmmm. It would certainly require much less effort if that were the case. There would be no struggling through our own emotional baggage to do it. Honoring great people would not take much emotional energy at all because our hearts would be so willing. Something in the human spirit longs to openly shout approval for the so-called good guys. Yet if we only honored the good guys, it would require no faith, and we know that it is impossible to please God without faith (Heb. 11:6).

Just a guess, but you probably wouldn't include your father in the good guy category, huh? He's not the shiny trophy you would display for all the world to see, is he? You know better. You know what he's done. Rather, you know what he's done *to you*. You may be able to consider forgiving him, but the audacity of anyone daring to suggest *honor* and *him* in the same sentence? Well, that is absurd!

Call me absurd. Here goes. I would like to suggest that you honor him. Is your face hot? Are your ears turning red? Is your heart pounding? Your stomach in your throat? How dare she? How dare little old me propose such a thing?!! Choke. Gag. Wretch! *Honor the man I can barely think of forgiving?*

Yes, girls, that is precisely what I am asking of you.

Before blowing a gasket, you need to understand what it means to honor him and why you should do it.

Honoring your father is something that you need to do for *yourself* — just like forgiveness. I believe it will help another piece of you heal. It will enable you to release a little more bitterness. Honoring him will allow you to free yourself from emotions that are destroying you inside.

I believe you can honor your dad by the way you live your life. Do not live your life just to spite him. Live your life in spite of what he taught you, or didn't teach you. You can walk in this world despite the challenges that he knowingly, or unknowingly saddled you with. Be a woman of honor "that it may go well with you" (Deut. 12:28; NKJV).

One of the best ways to honor your father, and one of the greatest leaps of faith you can take in that relationship, is to write a tribute. Write a declaration to him, and to the world, of the things that he has done right, and the reasons you love him.

God's fifth commandment, "Honor your father and mother . . ." may be one of the most profound in Scripture.

Daddy, Do You Love Me?

Indeed, I believe that there are penetrating and unforeseen benefits that are inextricably linked to one's obedience to this command. The best gift you can give your parents is the gift of honor.

Over the last decade, hundreds of people have written to describe how they took my advice and wrote a special Tribute to their parents. These treasured documents of love and appreciation have been used by God to bring blessing and even healing to many families. . . . Wherever you are in your relationship with your parents, I encourage you to write a Tribute. It may be one of the most profound, mysterious, and incredible experiences of your entire life.[3]

— Dennis Rainey

Now I know from experience the swarm of emotions that come along with the challenge to write a tribute to your father. I put it off for years. It is overwhelming and it is emotional. I will even go so far as to say that it is scary.

Both authors of this book have written tributes to their fathers, and it is the first time they have ever done so. After years of faith, forgiveness, and even restoration, they had never put their words on paper. Halfway through this book they set the task of writing aside, and chose to speak from the heart, directly to their fathers. It was incredible. Neither author had felt anger or animosity toward their fathers in a very long time. Both had forgiven their dads and found restoration. Their lives were on new tracks and they were reaping the rewards of faith and forgiveness. Still, something changed when they wrote these tributes. Another layer of the onion was peeled back, revealing new tenderness, new love, and new grace. God honors His Word, and there is indeed a blessing that comes with obedience.

For Shelby's Father
One "Punkin's" Tribute

Dad, where do I start? Our relationship has come so far in the last few years. For that, I am eternally thankful. We both know that the past isn't the prettiest part of our story. But, I can say with no doubts, the present is much more beautiful than I could have imagined. My heart smiles when I think of you. I am so excited that my children will know their Grandpa Dale and be loved by him. I hope they get to giggle and play with their goofy Grandpa for many years to come.

Ariel Allison and Shelby Rawson

As much as I hated it at the time, I can look back and laugh at the "afro" you gave me when you fixed my hair. Do you remember that? When I was four, you fixed my super curly hair with the blow dryer. It was huge!!

Even though I think I may have mortified you, I look back fondly at our bike rides. I remember sitting on the seat of your ten speed while you pedaled. I accidentally stuck my foot in the spoke and went head over heels to the ground. With blood on my chin, I walked home wailing something like "Why did you do this to me, Daddy?" What can I say? I was three. Who knew that the neighbors might get the wrong idea? Sorry about that, Dad! (I suppose I get a little chuckle out of it to this day.)

I will never forget the house on Chauncey Street. We used to have so much fun playing there. I met my first buddy Jake right around the corner. We used to have the best time playing in the leaves and in his cool "tree house." You came up with some pretty silly games like throwing dough balls at your homemade target on the refrigerator, and spit-wad fights. I especially loved taking all the cushions off the old, green couch and doing flips. And it wasn't a weekend without a trip in the TransAm to Grandpa and Grandma's house. I loved sliding across the backseat and bouncing in the air as we drove over the railroad tracks. Then we would arrive at my favorite destination, Grandpa and Grandma's farm.

You helped me learn how to play basketball and attempted to teach me golf (still haven't picked up the clubs!). You introduced me to the delicacy of fried bologna — and that you could put it on pizza! Thanks to Grandma, you also had a taste for baking. The turtle cake you made for my birthday is still vivid in my mind. I remember how you would strum your guitar and sing. I am now married to a man who does the same thing.

The giggles. You could give me the giggles like nobody else. I cherish the fact that I have a goofy dad who loves being silly and coming up with crazy names like "skunklebutter." Because of that, I love to be nutty for my own daughter. Just like you, I give my sweet girl the giggles.

Dad, you didn't have to say you were sorry or ask forgiveness, *but you did.* There are more fathers out there than I can count who would not and will not do the same thing. Those dads are depriving their daughters of a precious gift that I was able to receive from you. You took a step toward me with no guarantee of my response. *Thank you.*

Daddy, Do You Love Me?

Thank you for telling me I am pretty, smart, and talented. Thank you for never hanging up the phone without saying, "I love you, punkin." For opening up your house to my family any time we come back home and cooking meal after meal, I am grateful.

What is so near and dear to my heart this minute are the words I am able to write because of you. When I told you about the book, I was scared out of my wits. How did you respond to a book that would be airing the dirty laundry of our relationship? You excitedly and enthusiastically told me you were proud of me. You didn't hesitate. The blessing on our book came easily from your lips. Instead of blowing your top and trying to control my writing to save your face, you said, "Write whatever you need to write."

Months later, when I was in the thick of our book I hit a road block. My hands were practically frozen as I tried to type the words regarding some of my painful times with you. I didn't think I could do it. So, anxiously with my heart pounding, I called you. I could not manage to bring up the subject of the book, but you did. In total frankness I told you that I was stuck. You immediately asked if it was because of you . . . if I was worried that what I wrote would devastate you, and you went on to say that you could "take it." "Don't worry about me." In tears, I confessed that I was scared. Once again, you did not waver in your reassurance. "Don't be scared, Shelb. I know there is going to be hard stuff in this book. Say whatever you need to say. No matter what happens, you are my daughter and I'm going to love you. Don't be scared. Write your book."

As I pen these words, tears run over my face. Dad, you unfettered my wings and told me to soar. Not only does my Heavenly Father run to me with arms wide open, but so do you . . . so do you.

And now, Dad, I *know* you love me.

Love always,
Shelb

For Ariel's Father
"Water in the Face"

Dad, our relationship often resembled troubled waters. Maybe you had an inkling of that right from the start when Mom was in labor with me, and her water broke right in your face. Kinda gross, but pretty darn funny as well! You always said that if we'd been Native American, you would have named me, "Water in the Face." As I got older, I'm sure you

Ariel Allison and Shelby Rawson

felt like that is all I ever gave you, but I remember it to this day and it makes me smile.

I am just so thankful that there was more to our relationship than that. I have incredible memories of you.

I remember running around the house laughing hysterically while the "Tickle Monster" chased me. It is a game I play with my own children almost every day.

I remember how desperately you loved the word of God, and I am so thankful that you passed that love on to me. It is the greatest gift you ever gave me, and one that has guided my life.

I will never forget sitting in *Michael's Kitchen* and drinking hot chocolate with the whipped cream piled so high it always fell right off the mug and onto the table. You always bought me a "Long John" donut to go along with it. Several years ago I took my husband back to that restaurant and broke into tears right there at the table as I thought of that wonderful memory.

It is no mystery to me or anyone else why I love pens the way I do. You always had a pocket protector full of them. I don't know how you did it, but you always found the pen with the brightest color and the smallest tip. I was fascinated with them, and I constantly find myself buying pens, if for no other reason than they remind me of the ones you had.

I know we had our issues, and I know we butted heads for most of my life. Yet it is with no small amount of thankfulness that I can say you never hit me. You never called me a name. You never degraded me or made me feel stupid. When I was screaming insults at you, you bit your tongue. Your showed far more grace to me than I ever showed toward you.

Thank you for encouraging me to write. Even as a small child I would bring my stories to you and you fed my growing desire to put pen to paper. Not only that, but you introduced me to the legends of literature, and taught me to love the written word. Because of you I know C.S. Lewis, George McDonald, John Graves, and Ernest Hemmingway. You were always proud that your daughter was a writer, and I know that even though this book is about our struggles as father and daughter you would be so proud of me for being a published author. I know that you would not be afraid of a single word written on these pages, because we discussed it all before I lost you.

Your favorite song was the bluegrass classic "I'll Fly Away." I laugh every time I think of you clapping your hands and hopping around on

Daddy, Do You Love Me?

one foot while you belted out the words. You simply could not stand still while it was being played and when we sang it at your funeral, I found myself wanting to dance for you. I knew you were smiling.

I miss you, Dad. I miss you so much that sometimes I feel like my heart is going to explode. I am weeping as I write this because I would trade everything I own for just a few more minutes with you. I miss everything we didn't have in our relationship and even more than that, I miss what we did have.

I am always caught off guard by the intensity of the emotions that assault my heart when I open it up to memories of you. I remember you every time I look in the mirror. I have your jaw, your legs, and your "motor mouth." I have your temper, but I also have your ability to love the people in this world that no one else will. In a thousand ways I am my father's daughter, and I am so thankful for that. After a lifetime of living with you, longing for you, and wrestling with you, I can, in all honesty, say that I am proud to be the daughter of James Lee Allison. I am proud to be *your* daughter. I am proud that the last name you gave me graces the cover of this book (with the blessing of my husband). I have always thought it was the most beautiful last name a girl could possibly have.

I am forever grateful for the gift you gave me just hours before you died, and how you led me to the foot of the Cross in worship. I am thankful for the words of affirmation and love you sealed our relationship with. I know that one day I will step into the other side of eternity and you will be waiting for me and we will be able to pick up right where we left off, in worship, together. Just as it should be.

I love you, Daddy, and I know that you love me, too.

Your little firecracker,

Ari

LEAPING ON YOUR OWN

Taking your own leap of faith in honoring your father with a written tribute may take you 15 minutes or it may take you 15 years. I know well the deep pain rooted in many father-daughter relationships and am not ignorant to the fact that it can be very difficult to step out and move toward a dad that has wounded you terribly. The issue is not how long it takes you to do it, but that you are constantly moving forward with willingness.

Again, Dennis Rainey has granted permission to use his wisdom and his writing to explore this area of honoring our fathers. He guides us specifically through the process of writing a tribute, both the reasons for it and the ways in which it needs to be done. You will find the guidelines for writing a tribute at the end of this chapter. Many of you are going to skip over it for now, and that is okay. Just know that there will come a day in your life that you will need to go back and read those pages. I fully believe that your heart will not be able to move on until you have obeyed God by honoring your father. I recommend honoring him by writing a tribute because it is a formal document through which your faith is put into action. No one will tell you it is easy and no one can do it for you. This is your call to action. It is another step on the journey you are traveling, not the final destination.

Ariel's Thoughts

There have been several chapters in this book that have been particularly hard for me to write, and this is right up there at the top of the list. I was never good at honoring my dad. I purposefully dishonored him for much of my life. To make matters even worse, I taught my younger brother and sisters how to tear him down. I did it in front of my family and I did it in front of strangers. By the time I turned 16 I had earned a reputation for being a foul-mouthed, rebellious brute. My friends could not believe the things I got away with saying.

I am not proud of it. Two of my sisters are still in their teens and I find myself trying to undo the damage that I have done. They are fighting their own battles with a father who is no longer alive and I hate that I threw gasoline on those fires. Don't think for a moment that words don't matter. They will follow you to the grave, both the good and the bad.

There was a point in my life, however, when God convicted my heart and I knew that I was wrong. Here I was, the one who was doing the damage to our relationship, and it was a horrible feeling.

Even in my early twenties, as a married woman, my husband would pull me aside at family gatherings and gently reprimand me for the way I was treating my father. Even though I wanted to act differently, I just didn't know how. My behavior toward him had been wretched for so long that I felt powerless to change it.

The process was not easy. So I started with saying nothing. During the last six months of his life I took my infant son and visited with him once a week. I sat on the couch next to him and I just listened to what he had to say. Quite honestly, I was not interested in military tactics or presidential elections at the time. I wanted to talk about other things, but I chose to listen to what he had to say, and I was amazed by what I found. My father had a knack for tying current events into relevant discussions. It just took him a *really* long time to get to the point. It would always take over an hour of my listening before he got around to the important stuff.

I learned to sit and let my father speak to me. I didn't roll my eyes or huff my breath like usual. I just listened.

It may not seem like a major step, but for me it was important.

Then I practiced saying the things I needed to say with humility instead of anger. I knew that I had such a short time left with my dad, and there were things that I did not want to say over a grave. So I taught myself how to approach him with respect as my father, but also with gentleness and honesty. The last six months of his life we actually had some amazing conversations. I had to sit through a lot of small talk to get there, but it was wonderful when we went beneath the surface and connected heart to heart.

Just as I was beginning to learn what being a daughter is all about, he died. He was gone. Just gone. The relationship I had struggled with my entire life was over, and I couldn't have felt more empty. There was no satisfaction in being a fatherless daughter, and none in the absence of our struggle.

Even as I started to enjoy the process of discovering my dad, I no longer had the opportunity. But I knew there was one last thing God wanted me to do.

Before he passed, I felt that God was calling me to stand up at his funeral and honor him, publicly, officially, and it was me, of his six children, that needed to do it. Of everyone in his family, I had the most reason not to do it, but I was the one that needed to.

So I did, and it felt *good*. In front of 200 people I was able to honor my father for the things he had done right. And it was right for me to do it. I told of how he loved the Word of God and how he imparted that love to me. I told of his compassion for those in society that no one else cared for. I told of his sense of humor. I told of his great love for sharing the gospel. I told of his ability to keep a promise. He said "until death do us part," and he meant it. As I prepared his eulogy, it occurred to me that even though our struggle had been great, he gave me one of the best gifts possible: a home that stayed intact.

That was the last page in the last chapter of my relationship with my dad. All of my life I'd been looking for my "happily ever after," but what I got instead was far more valuable. I got a "well done good and faithful servant" (Matt. 25:21). I obeyed. I honored my father. I was freed of the emotional bondage that had haunted me my entire life. And you know what? I didn't stand in front of all those people and lie. Everything I said about my father that day was true. I padded nothing. I celebrated the good things about my father. I celebrated him, honestly and freely.

I said goodbye to my father on a Thanksgiving evening, and that day has become about far more than turkey for me. It has become a day that I quiet my heart and thank God for my father. Each year I try to honor him on that day, if not out loud, then at least in my heart.

One of the last things that I said to my dad was that Ashley and I intended to name our next son after him. Little did I know that I would soon have the opportunity. I got pregnant three months after my father passed away, and soon gave birth to our little James Parker. Every time I write his name or say it out loud I remember his namesake. The things that my father did right in his life are the qualities I pray my son will have.

Shelby's Thoughts

I think, for some of us, the thought of honoring the man who inflicted many of our deepest wounds sounds a bit more like torture than a true commandment from God — especially if this man still treats you like the gum he found on his shoe in the middle of July. If you are greeted with that *warmth and sensitivity* from your father, I can completely understand your overwhelming lack of enthusiasm. Yuck!

However, you are not someone's chewed up, spewed out, dirt-encrusted piece of Bubble Yum! I can happily confess that I'm not a masticated wad of gum, either. We are women made with splendor, beauty, tenderness, and lots of emotion. We are not pieces of trash just waiting to stick to someone's shoe. It was by no accident or mistake that we were made. What's more, we were never meant to be tossed carelessly to the curb for someone to trample on. We have worth. *You* are worthwhile — no matter how your dad has treated you.

So I speak to you as a woman who is worthy of love and respect. You can do it. You are capable of mustering a little bit of honor for a man who

Daddy, Do You Love Me?

may seem totally unworthy of honor. If not for your dad, do it for you. You need to recognize something positive you gained from the man who has broken his little girl's heart. Maybe he has a goofy sense of humor or a nice physique and you were blessed with one or both of those. Just try to recognize at least a little bit of the good things you got from him — even if he didn't intend for you to have them!

Obviously, I have been able to honor my dad. I'm certainly no expert at it. I fortunately have a father who wants a relationship with me. This makes it quite a bit easier to honor him. I will readily admit that it probably didn't take as much effort for me to do it as it will for those of you who have been physically and sexually abused through the actions of your fathers. With that being on the table, let me say that the first time my dad will read a tribute to himself will be when he reads this book. I cannot tell you that I wrote it and read it to him years ago. I just did it. Only a short time ago did I make the emotional effort to put it on paper.

But that's today. If I had been approached about honoring my dad ten years ago, these thoughts would be vastly different. Ten years ago, we weren't speaking, and I was trying my best to cope with the ache in my heart. Back then, honoring my dad would have sounded impossible. In the thick of my bleeding heart, I don't believe I felt emotionally capable of honoring my dad. It was a gradual process for me. I had to first walk through the process of recognizing the wounds, grieving, taking responsibility for my life, seeing him as a fallible person, and learning to forgive. That's a whole lotta stuff! In the midst of the process, I began taking steps to honor him with my words. Sometimes that meant saying no words at all.

You are probably in the middle of this. You are probably at the bottom of a hill and staring at the climb ahead of you. Running through it is not an option. Quitting in the middle of the journey will get you nowhere. The rough spots must be experienced. The strengthening of your heart must take place as you live and learn on this rough and rocky terrain. The one thing to keep in mind is the prize. Guess what? The prize is not your dad. He may not be waiting for you at the top of this hill . . . but your Heavenly Daddy will. Walk this road to rediscover your own beauty as given to you by the Master of all that is beautiful. I pray when you reach the top, you no longer reject the reflection in the mirror and you are confident of your Constant Companion.

Ariel Allison and Shelby Rawson

HOW TO WRITE A TRIBUTE

(reprinted with permission by *FamilyLife*)[4]

Writing a Tribute for Your Parents

Creating a written tribute to your parents — a formal document honoring them for what they've done right — may not be as difficult as you think. By reading the examples given in the book *Tribute*,[5] you can gain a greater understanding of the concept of honoring your parents.

Parents do not care whether you are a writer, a grammarian, or a spelling bee champion. They feel honored by the fact that you are speaking from the heart. You can accomplish this as you include special memories — those times of happiness, joy, celebration, and even pain and sadness that recapture how you felt as a child.

The best way to begin writing a tribute is to set aside a large chunk of time — perhaps an afternoon — to be alone with God and start putting thoughts and memories on paper. Here are a few suggested steps:

Step One: Prepare Your Heart

Spend some time in prayer and fellowship with God. Talk with Him, read His Word, and allow Him to search your heart. As Psalm 139:23–24 says, "Search me, O God, and know my heart; try me and know my anxious thoughts; and see if there be any hurtful way in me, and lead me in the everlasting way" (NAS95).

Here are a few questions to help you:

- Are you willing to look at your parents through the eyes of Christ?
- Are you looking to God, rather than your parents, for approval?
- Are your motives pure? Are you seeking to manipulate your parents through this gesture in any way?
- Are you prepared to honor them regardless of their response?
- Do you need to ask forgiveness for anything?
- Are you willing to forgive them for how they have hurt you?

Don't become introspective over these questions. The goal is to honor your parents, not to manufacture additional, unnecessary guilt in your life.

Step Two: Create a List of Memories

Your goal here is to collect as many memories as you can. Write down the good memories you have about your childhood — events, happy

Daddy, Do You Love Me?

occasions, interesting experiences with your family, things your parents taught you, and more. Don't be selective — you want to pull memories out of your mind and put them on paper.

You should be able to recall at least 10–15 specific good things about your parents. It may take a weekend (or a year) to bring them out, but usually those memories are stuffed in your brain.

You might want to start with an hour alone, just writing what you can remember. Then, over the next few weeks, carry around a notepad or some small cards and jot down anything that comes to mind. You will be surprised how, once you start, little things will spark memories — smells, sights, things people say, things your kids do.

The following questions should loosen a few rusty drawers in your brain:

- What was your favorite gift from your dad or mom?
- What memorable conversations do you recall having with your parents?
- Where did you go on vacations? What did you do?
- What was your happiest moment as a child?
- What did you enjoy doing with your dad or mom?
- What holiday traditions did you observe?
- What problems did your parents help you with as a child? As a teenager?
- What pets did they get for you?
- What activities did they encourage you to be involved in?
- What activities did they participate in with you (as a coach, teacher, etc.)?
- What was the funniest moment you experienced with your family?
- What special phrases did your family invent?
- What nicknames did people in your family have, and how did they earn them?
- What was your favorite birthday?
- What did other people think of your parents? How did other people react to your parents?

Ariel Allison and Shelby Rawson

- What do you admire about your parents?

- In what ways are you like them in your personality, skills, habits, etc.?

- How did your parents display affection for you?

- What character qualities did they model that have stayed with you?

- What values, learned from your parents, are you passing on to your children?

- What are any additional memories?

Step Three: Organize Your Material

If you are writing to both parents, one basic decision you will need to make is whether you want to write two individual tributes or one combined tribute. There's no right or wrong here — it all depends on the occasion and what you feel comfortable with.

There are many formats you can use to present your material, including a scrapbook, a book, a notebook, or a framed picture. The format you choose will help determine the length and look of your written material.

You may end up with dozens of items on your "memory list." You will need to reduce the number of items to fit whatever word length you have chosen for your final version, so now is the time to prioritize.

Go through the list and select the memories you feel are most important to include in the tribute. Remember, you do not need to include every memory that pops into your head, as in, "I remember going to the grocery store one time when I was a girl and you bought green beans." Some memories have no meaning! Just like picking only the freshest blooming flowers for a bouquet, choose the memories that are the most meaningful and vividly emotional to you.

Step Four: Write the Rough Draft

Don't worry about being fancy here — just tell the story as if you are talking to a friend.

To help guide you, here is a step by step outline:

1. Introduction

Explain why you are writing this tribute.

Example: "Too often we let our lives go by and we fail to let the ones who are most important to us know just how special

Daddy, Do You Love Me?

they are. You are special. There are many reasons I am thankful that you are my daddy."

2. What They Did Right

Turn each memory or character quality you have selected into a sentence or paragraph. The following examples show you can turn a single phrase into a sentence or paragraph by telling the story:

Example:

Memory/Character Quality: "Good provider . . . hard worker . . . went to work even when he was sick or when it was icy cold outside . . . paid my way through college. . . ."

Statement: "I never ever worried that I wouldn't have the things I needed or wanted, because you are such a hard worker. I can remember days you went to work even when you didn't feel good, and a few times you had to walk to work because of icy roads. And, unlike many parents, you paid my way through college."

3. Conclusion

Summarize your appreciation to your parents for the good they've done and how they have influenced you. This is also an ideal time to point to the future, to the relationship you want to continue to build with your parents, and to the legacy you are passing on to your own children.

Step Five: Put Together Your Final Draft

Take all the material you've put together on your worksheet and transfer it to some fresh paper. Look for ways to make improvements. Does everything make sense? Is the writing clear enough to understand what you are describing?

It might help to ask other people — your spouse or some friends — to look at your tribute because they may spot some problems you haven't thought of. They also can point out any grammatical or spelling errors you didn't catch.

Framing the Tribute

Once you have finished writing your tribute, it's time to give the gift to your parents. Take the document to a framing store and ask for advice on how to present it. Then create a clean version of the document, suitable for framing.

Here are a few options:

- If you have access to a computer with good word processing or desktop publishing software, set your document in the font style and size you desire. Then print on a laser printer.

- Have your document typeset by a local typesetter.

- Hire a calligrapher to give the document a classy look on parchment paper. Make sure the words are large and clean. In fact, this approach doesn't work well with longer documents unless you use a very large size piece of paper. Otherwise, calligraphy can be difficult to read.

- Decide if you want to add any photographs, artwork, or other memories to the document and plan accordingly.

Endnotes

1. Dennis and Barbara Rainey, *Moments Together For Couples* (Ventura, CA: Regal Books, 1995).

2. Gary Smalley and John Trent, *The Gift of Honor* (New York: Pocket Books, 1990).

3. Dennis Rainey, http://www.familylife.com/articles/article_detail.asp?id=486.

4. http://www.familylife.com/articles/article_detail.asp?id=486

5. Dennis Rainey with David Boehi, *Tribute: What Every Parent Longs to Hear* (Nashville, TN: T. Nelson, 1994).

Daddy, Do You Love Me?

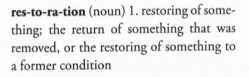

Authentic Restoration

res-to-ra-tion (noun) 1. restoring of something; the return of something that was removed, or the restoring of something to a former condition

Chapter 8

> Moreover, I will give you a new heart and put a new spirit within you . . . (Ezek. 36:26; NAS95).

> Lord, You give me strength
> To know when I'm weak
> And to see Your guiding hand.
> When I get down on my knees,
> Piece by piece, You make me whole again.
> — Stacie Orrico
> "Restore My Soul"

*I*t has been a long time since she wondered if he loves her. Her choices and her actions are no longer linked to that mystery. Last she heard, he was out there, somewhere, but she hasn't laid eyes on him in 30 years, not since her eighth birthday party. Something has changed in her heart, something deep and something precious. It was a long time coming, but its arrival was not silent. She woke one morning to the shouts of freedom in her heart. Freedom. Freedom from a crippling fear that she is not wanted. Freedom from the desire to punish the man who abandoned her. Freedom from the sorrow of being a fatherless daughter. Freedom, a sweet word indeed.

She knows who she is and every day she reclaims another piece of her dignity and self-worth. She is a daughter of the King. She is *His* little girl. She was made in the image of a Holy God, not in the image of a fallen father. She is loved. Oh yes, she knows for the first time in her life, that she is really and truly loved.

ANATOMY OF RESTORATION

Something was removed. The love and attention of your dad. A relationship with him. Some way, some how, the love you should have known from your daddy was taken away. What's more, the relationship you should have experienced with your father was eliminated. Gone. Removed.

Something needs to be returned to its former condition. Your heart. The heart of a child needs to be put back in its place. A little girl's hopeful heart calls for a strong rhythm inside your chest once again. Before the days of destruction, your heart had the faith of a child and unfettered dreams. Your forgotten heart is pleading to be returned to its former condition.

How? How do you replace what was removed? How do you restore your forgotten heart? You cannot turn back the clock to erase the ugliness any more than you can revisit those days and replace them with better ones. Even a beautifully restored life cannot accomplish that feat. So, can you replace the wrongs? Just simply get rid of them? No, brokenhearted one, you cannot.

Basically, I'm trying to tell you that you may need to try going in a different direction with your dad. You probably shouldn't try to start the same way you started way back when. You know, I cannot promise you that he will add any ingredients to your relationship. He may

Daddy, Do You Love Me?

be completely unwilling, incapable, or too dangerous (if his presence threatens your life in any way). You can emotionally rebuild your life, with or without your dad. His presence is not a required ingredient in the healing of your heart.

I realize that it doesn't seem fair, and pretty much stinks, if you have a father who is unwilling to play a part in the restoration of your relationship. Restoring his relationship with you is a privilege. If he chooses to forego that privilege, you are not responsible. Do not bear that burden. It is his alone to carry. You can only carry the weight of one conscience in this relationship, and that is your own.

When we think of being restored to our fathers, we probably all have the same mental image: a happy ending. For many, many of my readers, that is simply not going to happen. The reality of this fallen world is much more complicated than that. Sometimes fathers die, sometimes they are disinterested, and sometimes they stubbornly choose to continue down a path that leads them away from their daughters. There will be instances when all of our best efforts are for naught. In those cases, accepting that rejection, but not being bound to it, may be the greatest struggle of all.

WRITING YOUR STORY

The beautiful truth for each of us is that while we are still breathing, the story is not over. There is more to be written and we hold the pen. We make the choice. We have the freedom.

> Freedom is useless if we don't exercise it as characters making choices. . . . We are free to change the stories by which we live. Because we are genuine characters, and not mere puppets, we can choose our defining stories. We are co-authors as well as characters. Few things are as encouraging as the realization that things can be different and that we have a role in making them so.[1]
>
> — Daniel Taylor

Is your story going to be a tragedy or a triumph? Will it begin with heartache and end with hope? Will it be a picture of redemption and glory and strength? Or will it be the same as your father's story, sad and anticlimactic? Will the plot peter out in a confused mess of false starts and failed attempts? Or will there be a strong and consistent move toward a clear finish line? I ask you these questions, because you will

Ariel Allison and Shelby Rawson

determine the next chapter of your story. Not your father. You. That is freedom. That is empowerment. Regardless of what your father does in response to your growing faith and mending heart, you hold the key to your future.

SMALL CHOICES MAKE A BIG DIFFERENCE

By now you are probably eager for some practical advice. How does a distanced relationship begin to grow close? What can you do to move toward your father?

The good news is that the small, seemingly insignificant things may make the biggest difference in your relationship with your dad. Obviously, each relationship is unique, but I believe there are some universal truths that apply to each of us.

Remember him. Remember him on Father's Day, on Christmas, on his birthday. Let him know that you think of him. Seek him out. Start somewhere. Make it clear that you want something more for your relationship. At the beginning, all this may mean is sitting next to him at a family gathering and simply having a conversation. It may mean calling him for the first time in years, or if you can't find the courage to call, then write. It may mean seeking out a father you have never known.

Start small. Take little leaps of faith. You don't necessarily need to pour your heart out in one fell swoop. Baby steps. With each move forward, gather your strength and gain courage. Remember that this is a worthy cause, and one that will change your life. As Dennis Rainey says, "Honoring parents should be a direct result of our faith in God."[2] Pursuing your dad is evidence of your faith, and it is that faith that will guide you to rebuilding your relationship.

Restoration is an intensely personal thing, and it does not look the same for any two women. You know the authors of this book have stories on the opposite ends of the spectrum. One of them is fully restored to her father and is thriving in a new and healthy relationship. The other buried her father three years ago, and must seek out a different Father to soothe her heart. Both are fully restored, but the realities of that restoration are very different for each of them.

The responsibility for moving toward restoration lies on your shoulders. It is a turning of your heart toward your father. It is the recognition that he was sovereignly placed in your life, and that he holds a place of honor regardless of his actions toward you. It is the admission that having

Daddy, Do You Love Me?

a father is important. It matters. Ultimately, it is the willingness to do anything that God asks of you in this relationship with your father. Some of that is blatantly revealed in Scripture, and some of it will be unique to you and to your circumstances.

As you start this journey, it is imperative to remember that your real Father will guide you as you pursue your dad. Seek wisdom. Pray about how to approach your dad. Believe it or not, God wants you to be restored to your father even more than you do, but always, always keep in mind that even more than that, He wants you to be restored to *Him*.

RESTORING THE HEART FIRST

Your forgotten heart. You have concealed it, hoping that it would be well protected if you kept it buried. Let it breathe. Allow the hopes and dreams of a lost little girl to take flight once again. I know it isn't easy. In fact, it's scary. You're probably not too sure that you can handle the possible blow of having your hope deferred, but if you don't let your hope override your fear, then you are allowing your heart to stay trapped in the same lonely prison it's known for far too long. It is time for your heart to be restored.

It's time for the rebuilding of a relationship. Maybe your dad is willing, maybe he's not. Either way, reconciling that relationship alone won't replace or return all that was ruined in you. There is only one way to make that happen. It's a God thing. He can replace the broken heart with one that is healed. What's better, you can restore your relationship with your perfect Dad. True redemption can occur no matter what happens with men on earth because it takes place through the Father. He wants a relationship with you. The question is: do you want a relationship with Him?

Restoration begins in the heart with an acknowledgement that God is your real Father, and that He knows what is best for you. You can never be truly restored to your earthly dad without first connecting with your Heavenly Father.

I have been whispering, sometimes shouting, in your ears that God is waiting for you. He longs to have His little girl back in His arms. He'll never force you. The arms of grace and mercy are open to you for the embrace of a lifetime. The feet of the Father run toward His lost little girl. He lingers outside your heart — all you need to do is speak His name and invite Him in.

Ariel Allison and Shelby Rawson

Invite the Father to come into your heart and into your life. Fall on your knees. Fall into His arms and receive the blessing of His comfort and the security of His Son.

Shelby's Thoughts

I am not going to pretend that I haven't been blessed by the restoration of my relationship with my dad. God answered that prayer for me beyond my imagination. However, it did not take place over night. We didn't have a phone conversation and bing, bang, boom — perfect restoration! At first, it was a little awkward. Conversation didn't come easily. Hanging out with my dad made me nervous. I wasn't too sure what we would say. I would get anxious at the thought of one of us saying the wrong thing and causing more hurt feelings.

I would venture to say that I stayed guarded for quite a while. It is kind of like diving into the water for a swim. You used to do it quite a bit, but kept getting hurt. Eventually, you become injured to the point that you wouldn't go near the water. One day, you decide that swimming is too important for you to avoid it. So you go back to the water. At first you sit on the edge of the pool and hang your feet in. After a while, you climb down the ladder at the shallow end — away from harm. You're only up to your waist. The deep end is waiting for you. That's where the real action is — and you know it. That's also where you got hurt. Do you stay shallow, or go deep? Do you play it safe and boring, or take the plunge? You know it's a choice. My dad wasn't going to get any closer to me in the shallows. In time, I went for the deep.

Our relationship started down a new path over six years ago. It has been in the last couple of years that I have begun to feel really comfortable whenever we're together. Now, I can say the deep end is just another pool of water. It's not daunting. It's inviting. I look forward to conversations with my dad. I get excited about spending time with him and I sincerely believe that he wants to spend time with me.

I could have taken another path. I could easily have refused his invitations to come to his house and stay. If I had done that, I could have avoided ever feeling uncomfortable or worrying about what might happen or not happen. Believe me, that is a mental battle that I have fought more times than I can count! But, for once in my life, I did something that made me squirm a little. Instead of avoiding, I acted. I chose to hope. For once, I fought my fears and found a little faith.

Daddy, Do You Love Me?

Something I must confess to you is that at the beginning of our newly budding relationship — I broke his heart. The bridge between us wasn't too strong just yet as I was planning my wedding. So on my wedding day, I chose another man to walk me down the aisle . . . while my dad watched from a pew. Until recently, I didn't have a clue what that did to my dad's heart. He had watched two daughters marry without the pleasure of guiding them into the arms of their husbands. My heart feels heavy as I think of the pain I unintentionally caused him.

Yes, my relationship with my dad has been restored. I consider myself one of the lucky ones. My dad was not necessarily obliged to restore our relationship. He made a choice, too. He wanted a relationship with me. Luckily, my heart was at a place to receive the opportunity of restoration with him.

Not all dads will make the same choice. Some of them will be just plain stubborn and stupid. I know that they may very well choose their pride over their daughters. If that is your dad, it makes me angry for you. If you were willing and he was unwilling, good for you and bad for him. And history repeats itself — he is missing out on the gift of his daughter.

I did not restore this relationship by myself. For me, it took a "cord of three strands" to mend our relationship (Eccles. 4:12). I couldn't do it by myself. I wasn't strong enough or brave enough to battle my fears and subdue the voices in my head reminding me of the past. Thankfully, I know a Savior who doesn't expect me to be the strong one. He knows my weaknesses — and that's a good thing. "[His] grace is sufficient for [me], for [His] power is made perfect in weakness" (2 Cor. 12:9; NIV). In my surrendering and admitting that I was afraid and couldn't do it alone, He was there. His strength completed my own. His power moved me to act. "For when I am weak, then I am strong" (2 Cor. 12:10; NIV).

I did not walk one step of my journey to restoration alone. No matter how lonely I felt in my room, my car, or in a crowd, my Father was with me. Even when I was screaming at Him for the path I had to walk, He didn't leave. He listened to my ranting and raving and continued on right beside me. God knew my heart couldn't quite understand that He was a loving Father just yet, so He pressed on. And, He still does. He still walks with me, reminding me, and revealing to me more and more that *in Him* I find my perfect Father-daughter relationship. With Him, perfect restoration can be found.

Ariel Allison and Shelby Rawson

No matter what life has dealt you, restoration can be yours. You just need to know who it is that is always waiting for you and walking with you.

Ariel's Thoughts

I won't pretend that it isn't hard for me to watch Shelby enjoy a newfound relationship with her dad. As a matter of fact, I am jealous. And I have told her as much.

You see, I love stories. God has always spoken to me through stories. Shelby's story speaks so much about the heart of God and about healing. I am envious of that. My story does not resemble hers at all. Mine is lonely at times. I walk it by myself because I no longer have a living father. My struggles and triumphs are just that: mine. Not "ours." My father and I don't sit on the porch and discuss where God has brought us. Yes, I can share them with you, and yes, my husband is with me each step of the way, but I will never have the connection that only a father can give. Not with James Lee Allison anyway. I long to hug my dad and share tender moments. I long to have conversations full of meaning. I wish I could know how I made him feel during those years that I pushed him away. I wish I had the opportunity to start over. I wish I still had my father.

On almost every page of this book we have pressed home the reality that we have a Father even greater than the man who gave us life. I believe that with every bone in my body. Yet my confession is that I often have a hard time *feeling* that truth. My journey toward restoration is one of faith, and it is one where I have often struggled. But know this: it is also one where God has spoken to me in profound ways. The surprises have been numerous and delightful.

It is often in the most simple ways that God has gripped my heart. A recent example happened on a trip to Texas where my husband and I met up with his old pastor and mentor. Tom had only met me once before, yet he embraced me with the most powerful and tender hug I have ever received. I could barely hold back my tears because every fiber in my being said that is what a father's hug ought to be, and God whispered to my heart that is exactly what He is offering — a perfect embrace where I am safe and loved, strong arms that will protect, and a heart that has room for me. I took yet another step toward my Father.

I long for a daddy, and I believe that I will until the day I die. I was meant to be the delight of my father, not for a moment on his deathbed,

Daddy, Do You Love Me?

but for the entirety of my life. This longing that I endure has caused my heart to hunger deeply for my real Father. Yet I am easily satisfied with my progress, and that is not a good thing. I once heard that God is easily pleased, but He will never be satisfied with our steps of faith. He wants so much more *for* us than we will ever know we are capable of having. He wants so much more *of* me than I have ever dreamed of giving.

The redeeming of a relationship is characterized by faith. I have on my mantel a picture of me in my wedding dress, being led down the aisle by my father. At the time, I almost asked another man to do it because, in my arrogance, I felt as though my father had not earned the right to give me away. Yet I knew in the depths of my heart that he was the only man who ever could. So in faith I gave him that honor, and today I thank God that I did. He never had the chance to walk his other three daughters down the aisle. When one of my sisters married a year ago, it was my husband who stood in that gap. I know that God spoke to my father's heart by giving me away, but it is I that have gained the greater blessing through the years.

So you see, it is the smallest, seemingly insignificant things that build a bridge from one heart to another. Redemption happens in the small choices of daily life. It is the choice to let him give you away at your wedding, and it is the choice to send a card on Father's day. It is a choice riddled with faith. Sometimes it is the smallest choices that require the most faith.

Am I restored? Yes. Both to my dad, and to my God. I have surrendered my heart to my true Father, and I have done everything He has asked me to do in relationship with my dad. My heart has been changed. I no longer harbor grief, anger, and disappointment. I have seen my father through the eyes of Christ, and I have received him — the good, the bad, and the ugly. He was not perfect, but neither am I. I have learned to love and respect him, and that may be the biggest miracle of all, because I feared I never would.

Endnotes

1. Daniel Taylor, as quoted by John Eldridge, *Wild At Heart: Discovering the Secret of a Man's Soul* (Nashville, TN: Thomas Nelson, 2001).

2. Dennis and Barbara Rainey, *Moments Together for Couples* (Ventura, CA: Regal/Gospel Light Books, 1995), devotions for April 28, 29, and 30.

Ariel Allison and Shelby Rawson

For the Boys

I know a girl,
She puts the color inside of my world
 And she's just like a maze
 Where all of the walls continually change,
  And I've done all I can
  To stand on the steps with my heart in my hand.
Now I'm starting to see
Maybe it's got nothing to do with me.
 Fathers be good to your daughters.
 Daughters will love like you do.
  Girls become lovers who turn into mothers,
  So mothers be good to your daughters, too.
      — John Mayer
      "Daughters"

Chapter 9

They'd only been married a little while — a few weeks maybe — when it started. Or maybe it all began when they were engaged. She can't remember the exact time frame, but she can remember the feelings. The tension, and the surprise that she was already squirming uncomfortably in her new marriage.

It's not supposed to be like this, she thought. *We're newlyweds. Aren't we supposed to be blissfully happy for a little while? The tension and the fighting shouldn't kick in for at least a few more months. It's only been a couple of weeks.*

Painfully, she recalls the panic that seized her as she thought about her worst fears coming true. Was her marriage doomed to be just like her parents'? Had she chosen to spend the rest of her life with a man who was going to reject her just like her dad? The mere thought of more pain in her heart drove her to tears as she pleaded with God. *Please, God, please. No more pain. I can't take it from the only man I've ever given my heart to. Please make him tread softly. Help, Lord.*

On those days, she would do her best to keep silent. She was scared to death that her words would cause another argument. She had begun to convince herself that it was only a matter of time before he would get sick of her and leave.

What man would want to stay married to a woman who isn't able to open up to him? Or can't have a discussion without tensing up, getting defensive, and attempting to avoid a potential conflict? She felt fairly confident that he had married a freak who didn't know how to have a real relationship.

It didn't help matters that he didn't know how to respond to her insecurities. At first he would try to be patient, but after several rounds of crashing head first into her walls and being laid flat by her baggage, he'd explode. She had no idea what to do with his reaction. So she did what she knew, she withdrew and wept — alone. Often she would go into the closet, curl up on the floor, and sob — much like she did as a little girl. Only, as a little girl, she would hide away in the cubby hole under her bunk bed.

He would always come to her and apologize. Then he would attempt to explain to her that he just wanted her to talk to him without getting defensive and to have a serious conversation without it sending her into a tailspin. He needed her to connect with him emotionally and for her to put a little trust in him. In the end, he would do his best to remind her that he wasn't going anywhere and that he was committed to her for the long haul. "I know that you have never seen a man stick by you, but that's not me. I get angry, say things I regret . . . and I'm sorry. I love you, but I can't be Jesus for you. I can't be everything to

Daddy, Do You Love Me?

you — only He can. And I know that God is going to get us through this. I am praying that He will help you learn how to trust me. *I am not your dad. . . .*"

No, he wasn't her dad. Yet the same fears she'd come to know so well as a daughter plagued her mind as a wife. She hated it. She hated that the life she'd known with her dad was affecting the new life she was trying to form with her husband. She hated that the one man on this earth she wanted to cling to was the one man she pushed away.

He's not my dad. He's not any of the men who stumbled into my childhood.

Her body felt heavier than her heart as she looked back on the first part of their marriage and realized several years later she still struggled. She can see it more clearly now. Some days she can recognize when she is making her husband pay for someone else's mistakes . . . and some days she can't. A sigh empties from her chest as she yearns for her heart to finally be free. One fear at a time. One conflict after another. She knows one day she will allow him to love her. One day, she will believe in his words and she won't respond to him with fear. Shutting her eyes, she reminds herself again, "He is not my father."

WHAT YOU DON'T KNOW ABOUT YOUR WIFE

Isn't that how you feel, guys? You've married this girl and you love her. You really do, but as John Mayer put it, "I've done all I can, to stand on the steps with my heart in my hand. Now I'm starting to see, maybe it's got nothing to do with me."

Sometimes you lay in bed with her, so close you can feel her heart beat, but you know she is not even there. She has withdrawn to that place. She does it every time you have an argument. All you want is to hold her in your arms and love her, not just make love *to* her, you want to love *her*. You want to love away all of her pain, and you just can't understand why she doesn't leave that pain in the past. Why did she bring it with her when you got married? It drives you crazy. It makes you mad. None of this is your fault, but you are paying the price, and you become angry at her. She's lashing out at you every time you try to pull the folds back and go deep. So you lash back. You're tired and you're worn out from the difficulties you've had with this relationship.

What you may not understand is that she is on the other side of that wall and she feels paralyzed. She's doing the "Come hither, go away" thing

Ariel Allison and Shelby Rawson

and she doesn't even know why. Believe it or not, she desperately wants you close. She is afraid that the closer you get, the more vulnerable she becomes. Oh, the blows she took from her father hurt, there is no doubt about that. She would be the first to admit it, but what she is truly afraid of is you. You. You hold in your hand, more so than any man, the ability to crush her spirit to the point of no return. She knows that, even though she may not be able to admit it, or put it to words.

As John Eldridge says in *Wild At Heart*:

> Every woman can tell you about her wound, some came with violence, others came with neglect. Just as every little boy is asking one question, every little girl is, as well . . . the deep cry of a little girl's heart is *am I lovely*? Every woman needs to know that she is exquisite and exotic and *chosen*. This is the core to her identity, the way she bears the image of God. *Will you pursue me? Do you delight in me? Will you fight for me?* She has taken a wound as well. The wound strikes right at the core of her heart of beauty and leaves a devastating message with it*: No. You're not beautiful and no one will really fight for you. . . .* her [wound] almost always comes at the hand of her father."[1]

MAKING MUSIC TOGETHER

God did not design the father-daughter relationship to mirror His image. He said, "A man shall . . . be joined to his *wife; and they shall become one flesh*" (Gen. 2:24; NAS95, emphasis added). One! Because of the great privilege you have before God, you alone have more influence over her heart than any person alive. There is nothing that her father could have done to her that God can not heal through you. Notice I did not say that *you* could heal her. I said that God can heal it *through* you.

An example of this healing occurs in the classic poem, *Touch of the Master's Hand* by Myra Brooks Welch:

> 'Twas battered and scarred, and the auctioneer
> thought it scarcely worth his while
> to waste much time on the old violin,
> but he held it up with a smile.
> "What am I bid, good folk?" he cried.
> "Who'll start the bidding for me?

Daddy, Do You Love Me?

A dollar — a dollar — then two, only two.
Two dollars and who'll make it three?
Going for three" — but no.
From the room far back, a gray-haired man
    came forward and picked up the bow.
Then, wiping the dust from the violin
    and tightening the loosened strings, he played
    a melody pure and sweet as a caroling angel sings.
The music ceased, and the auctioneer,
    with a voice that was quiet and low,
    said, "Now what am I bid for the old violin?"
And he held it up with the bow.
"A thousand dollars and who'll make it two?
Two thousand dollars and who'll make it three?
Three thousand once, three thousand twice,
    and going and gone," cried he.
The people cheered but some of them cried,
"We do not understand, what changed it's worth?"
Quick came the reply:
"The touch of the master's hand."
And many a man with life out of tune,
    and battered and scarred with sin,
    is auctioned cheap to a thoughtless crowd,
Much like the old violin.

Your wife is the violin, you are the bow, and God is that Master whose hand is so gentle, but experienced, that He can take two totally different things and bring them together for profoundly beautiful music.

Isn't that what both you and your wife long for — the touch of the Master's hand? Your wife has music in her yet, though she often doesn't look much like it. You are the instrument through which it can be released.

She longs for the tender touch of one who knows her intimately. She longs to be played, not by manipulation, but by love. She longs to give her best. She wants someone to see past her scars and her tarnish, see her for who she really is, and to hope in all that she can be.

Women, that man you are married to (or will be married to one day) is the one God placed in your life, the bow, the one who brings the music forth. That man needs to know the value of this old violin. Not to say that we haven't made him endure more than his fair share of sour notes. Sometimes we have refused to share our music altogether. Sometimes we have deprived him of the privilege of enjoying us. Yet here we are, joined together, bow and violin, and there is a marriage between us that has the possibility of creating music so enchanting that the beauty will repair our damaged hearts.

You may wonder about the bow in your life. Does he know about those scars and tender spots? Does he try to force the music out? Is he playing you in the wrong way? Do you feel as though you could never make music with this man?

Men, do you get this? You cannot make music without her, and you cannot force yourself upon her, expecting results. There is a Great Musician, who knows that woman better than she knows herself. He alone can teach *you* how to bring her music forth. When was the last time you went back to the Master and asked Him to teach you? Have you allowed yourself to become a student of your wife, who knows the most intimate details of her heart? Have you forgiven her for her sour notes? Have you pursued her to the point of exhaustion, even if only to let her know that you are not like her father? Oh, I'm sure she doesn't respond at times. As a matter of fact, I'm sure she pushes you away and leaves you in the cold and you begin to understand why her dad made some of his bad choices. After all, it's tempting, isn't it? It's tempting to quit, to walk out, to give up, but you will never make music that way.

What your wife really wants to say, and may not have the courage to tell you, is, "Don't give up on me. I need you. I know it may not seem like that sometimes, but I need you. I'm scared of you. I am scared you will hurt me and leave me far worse off than my father ever did. I need you to be strong for me. I need you to be stronger than my dad. I need you to hold me and let me cry. I don't want you to fix me. We both know that you can't. I want you to love me. I mean really love me. Love me despite all my crap. Love me even though I don't deserve it. I need you to let God teach you what it means to be my husband. Not *a* husband, but *my* husband. Please, please, be patient with me. I am trying to reclaim the glory in my heart and I am trying to learn how to share that glory with you. I want to. My heart longs to make music with you. I just don't know how to sing. I am willing to let God use you to bring out the best in me. Just be gentle, please."

Daddy, Do You Love Me?

Maybe you know exactly what instrument you are and, therefore, how you need to be played. You have enough of a sense of self that communicating your needs to your husband isn't a challenge for you. Telling him how you feel and expressing your opinions is part of your everyday life. If this is you, that is wonderful.

Maybe this is not you. Maybe you can relate to the woman who trips over her words when it's time to talk to her husband. He initiates a conversation with you and inside you are forming knots of frustration, anxiety, and tension. Your husband can seem to spit out exactly what he wants to say while you flounder. The more he talks, the worse you feel. The more he tries to get a response from you, the less you want to respond. Your words become a prisoner in your brain, running through a maze like a rat on a hunt for cheese, and scrambling wildly to get to their final destination — your tongue. Perhaps you try to speak in the middle of the brain chase. The words that come out are not quite what you need to say. So your husband keeps talking. He asks questions. The rat scrambles more quickly now and focus becomes impossible. You begin to feel overwhelmed by what started out as a fairly simple, non-threatening conversation.

You may find yourself wondering in frustration. *Why on earth does this happen with your husband of all people? Why can you articulate your feelings with a girlfriend?*

Well, let's think about it for a minute. Has there ever been an important man in your life who validated your feelings and valued your opinion? If you were never able to express your thoughts and emotions to your dad, it affected your ability to communicate with men. If you were made to feel as though your words were insignificant and worthless by your father, then you learned to keep them to yourself. Deep down, you are scared to death to say how you truly feel because the one man you *chose* to love may invalidate your precious thoughts and emotions. Once upon a time, you learned that it wasn't safe to express yourself to the most important man in your life — your dad. Now, something inside you tells you it's not safe to put your feelings on the table for your husband. He's frustrated. You're paralyzed.

You may love thinking of yourself as a violin waiting only to be played by your husband's tender hand, and then you think, *Am I really a violin*? Do you know what instrument you are? Do you have a clue? If not, then how do you know how you are to be played? Can your husband figure out how to make his beautiful wife into a sweet melody if he doesn't know what he's playing? He's trying a pick. You are not a guitar. He tries his fingers. You're not a piano, either. He puckers his lips. You are definitely not a flute. Over and over he tries to play your song, but you, in your emotional confusion and paralysis, keep changing your tune. You are still trying to figure out what it is that makes you sing.

Truth be told, you feel trapped within yourself. There is a woman in there begging to be seen. To be known. To be safe in her exposure. And, yet, you remain. Stuck. Insecurity pulls you down. Fear keeps its thumb on you. Meanwhile, your dream of the picture of marriage is becoming hazier. The things you pictured yourself doing are slipping away from you because your feet are stuck in your muck — the muck that whispers to you every time you think you might move beyond the fear. *He will reject you. He isn't safe. His love is conditional, too. If you mess this up, he won't keep you around, either. You will never be good enough. Smart enough.* And he wins. Every time you listen to the whispers of the past, the Chief Liar gains ground in your life. Satan does a little dance knowing that all it takes is a few lies planted in your head and you are immobile.

So you remain. Defensive. Passive. Withdrawn. Addressing conflict is your arch rival. Shutting down is your hideaway. Within your walls, you make your dwelling place.

Guys, if you have just read what seems to be a description of your wife, please don't give up. There is still a little girl in the heart of the woman you have married. She was shut down emotionally and has never recovered. She truly doesn't know how to communicate her feelings to you because sometimes she isn't even sure what they are. Trying to pull them out of her probably makes her more anxious and less confident to speak. Describing her own thoughts and feelings feels foreign and scary to her. You are not just dealing with a grown woman. You are dealing with the tender injuries of a seven-year-old daughter. Tread lightly on her heart.

She wants so badly for you to hear her voice, but she may not have found it yet. It has been silenced so many times that she can barely recognize the sound of it. Your patience is probably already worn, but dig down. Gut this out. She needs her husband to be the one man in her life who finds her. She needs you to see her. She needs you, the man she chose to marry, to be safe. Do not run at her. Run to her. Meet her in her hiding place. Help her come out of the lonely darkness that she may at long last be encompassed by the embrace of the most important man in her life — you.

A WORD OF CAUTION

Isn't it beautiful? Just thinking of the healing touch that can come from the man we love is enough to lift our spirits. It's true, your husband can do more to restore your heart than any other living person, but do not, for one moment, make the mistake of thinking that he will meet all your needs. If you are single today, and you read those words, false hope will say that once you get married, everything in your heart is going to be okay. It simply isn't true. If you are married, you may know all too well that sometimes there is no healing in his touch.

Remember, the bow cannot play the violin on its own. It is held by the Master. There is a need and a longing in your heart that only the God of heaven can satisfy. Even women who had phenomenal fathers have a God-shaped hole in their hearts. Every woman who enjoys the tender touch of her husband still longs for what only God can give.

Ultimately, your confidence, your hope, your joy, and your sense of self-worth have to be rooted in God, and who He says you are, not in any mortal man, be it your father or your husband. God gives you your identity.

Pinning your hopes on your husband will do nothing more than create a clingy, needy, shallow woman. The man you married is also a broken man. There are things in his life that have wounded him deeply, perhaps even a blow from his own father. Together you traverse this road, and together you learn to make music. The two of you are only instruments, not the hand that plays them. For a healing melody to pour forth from your life, you have to be guided by the hand of the Master.

BROKEN VOWS, SHATTERED DREAMS

The reality for many women out there is that the man you married is very much like your father. He is not kind. He is not considerate. He has been dealt his own share of blows, both emotional and physical. Many of you reading this book are no longer married. Your Cinderella story died in the ashes of divorce. You know from experience that marriage doesn't fix everything. For you, it didn't fix anything. Redemption never came at the hands of your husband, only more pain and a greater

Ariel Allison and Shelby Rawson

disillusionment with men. Your stories are messy and complicated and you have not seen a happy ending. Love has been elusive and hope has been non-existent. You know that both the violin and the bow must be yielded to the Master. Sometimes the bow does not bend. It is harsh and abrasive. You also know that the violin often refuses to be played, the strings wound so tight that only sharp notes pour forth.

I would be naïve to assert that every woman finds her heart in the embrace of marriage. It simply is not true. The fact remains that all men, both fathers and husbands, are fallen creatures. As are we. It doesn't take two to tango, it takes three: husband, wife, and Master.

What hope then does the woman in a bad or broken marriage have? What does she cling to when her heart has died on the altar of disappointment? Simply this — to remember that the bow does not create the music. The bow does not bring the redemption. The bow does not fix the violin. It is the Master's hand that fixes, redeems, and creates. Above all, there must be a return to the Master, a yielding to that hand, and a willingness to let Him tell your story. Redemption begins with Him. There can be no pure music in your life until your heart has been tuned to Him.

Brokenness and beauty are tightly wound together. Hope and heartache are intimate friends. Singing and sorrow sway to the same rhythm. We are the broken. You are the healer. Jesus Redeemer, mighty to save.

A WORD TO FATHERS

Our society does not give fathers the credit they deserve. For some reason, it has become okay to bash dads. No, it has become *expected* to bash dads. Think about the shows we see on TV: *Married With Children*, *Roseanne*, *The Simpsons*, *That 70s Show* . . . the list is endless.

Our culture has deemed fathers, and men in general, to be useless, unnecessary, and ineffective. Our culture could not possibly be more wrong. Of both parents, I feel as though fathers are the anchor that keeps a family from drifting. The worth of a father is indescribable. The responsibility of fathers is overwhelming.

Obviously, this is not a book about mothers, and *yes* we are fully aware that mothers do their fair share of damage in a daughter's heart. That confession is a little less accepted in our world. Mothers tend to be on an ever-present pedestal as the saint of the family. In many cases, that isn't true. Perhaps another day we will delve into that discussion, but for the moment we are talking to you dads. There is no passing the buck to

174 *Daddy, Do You Love Me?*

your wife or ex-wife, girlfriend or ex-girlfriend. Today it is about you and what you are doing with the heart of your daughter.

Trying to capture and understand the heart of your daughter can be very much like trying to capture and understand the heart of your wife: elusive and frustrating. The fact is that women are mysterious and ever-changing creatures. There is no blueprint to her heart. One moment you have a bouncing toddler content to sit on your lap, and the next, a teen-age girl that doesn't want to be seen in public with you. That daughter of yours will keep you on your toes for the rest of her life. That being said, it may help to break things down a little.

The Child Daughter: The First Ten Years

We all know that there is nothing sweeter than seeing a little girl with her daddy. Somehow it just seems right. There is an essence of protection and delight when we see a father hold his daughter tenderly. Perhaps that is why there is such a betrayal when things go wrong. It is devastating. It is wrong on the most primal level.

The good news about the first ten years of your daughter's life is that it will never be easier to capture her heart than it is right now. She will never be more forgiving of your mistakes than she is today. She will never be more open to your efforts than she is during those years.

She comes from the womb in love with you. She is oblivious to your failings and your insecurities. Use that to your advantage. A little love goes a really long way right now, and a lot of love can secure her heart forever. It is yours for the taking.

While she is a small child, the greatest way to express love to your daughter is through physical touch. (It should go without saying that your touch is never, ever to be of a sexual nature. Ever.) A hug, a kiss, a stroke of her hair tells her that she is loved and protected. A piggyback ride through the park or holding her hand in the grocery store assures your little girl that she is treasured.

As she grows, it will become increasingly important for her to receive affirmation of her physical beauty. Every daughter born longs to know she is beautiful. She longs for that assurance in every fiber of her being. It is something placed by God in the heart of a woman. Her mother can tell her she is pretty and she may doubt the sincerity. If her father says it, she will believe it. She needs to know that you think she is the prettiest little girl that ever lived.

Ariel Allison and Shelby Rawson

Her self worth needs to come from the fact that she was created in the image of God (Gen. 1:26), not in *your* image. She needs to know there is great purpose in her life, and that purpose is rooted in the plan of a sovereign God.

Dads, you are in a unique position to help foster your daughter's identity. This is an incredible gift and amazing responsibility you have been given. Do not leave her identity up to teachers, coaches, and grandparents. She needs to be validated and affirmed by you in her choices, her character, and her activities. If your six year old is trying to do something for the first time, encourage her. If she is talented in a particular area, praise her. Her talents may not be obvious. You may need to take a genuine interest in her and look for them. You may even need to help her find her talent. Keep in mind, you do not get to decide what her talent will be. That is something out of your control. She may be really good at reaching out to people in love and making others feel special. Your daughter may be quite the little artist with her crayons. Running may be her thing. Whatever her talents and good qualities are, you should make a recognizable effort to applaud her. In doing this, you will be cultivating amazing growth in your daughter's heart. She will gain a sense of confidence that will stick with her the rest of her life. This is the same confidence she will need to say no to peer pressure and yes to the challenges that life throws her way. If you want your little girl to feel loved and accepted by her daddy, help her understand what a wonderful identity she possesses.

Did you ever stop to think that your little ballerina is going to grow up and face a world equipped only with what you give her? Are you supplying her with the tools to navigate this world we live in? Does she know that her purity is a precious thing not to be squandered? Are you modeling for her how a man should treat his wife? Is she protected from the dangers and the evils of this world that are desperately working to corrupt her?

Little girls grow up. It is a fact. As John Mayer put it, "Fathers be good to your daughters. Daughters will love like you do. Girls become lovers, who turn into mothers." What kind of mother is your little girl going to be?

That daughter of yours is going to marry a man one day, and the kind of dad you are is going to greatly affect that man's life. Have you ever stopped to think about the kind of wife you want her to be? Have you thought about what she will need to have a successful marriage? Are you

Daddy, Do You Love Me?

leaving her a legacy of divorce, anger, and bitterness? What is it exactly that you are giving to your daughter?

That is how the story goes. You have a few short years to capture the heart of your little girl. Because the fact is, they don't stay little for long. You blink your eyes and your little girl is someone's wife. She is no longer your little girl, she is someone's lover and someone's mother. The choices you make when she is little will determine whether or not she still wants to be your "little girl" later in life. Many daughters don't, and their fathers bear the burden for that.

The Adolescent Daughter:
Painfully Pubescent and Tumultuous Teens

I think most of us have heard a new daddy joke about greeting their baby girl's first date at the door with a shotgun and then proceeding to take him into a room all by his lonesome for a little chat. He cannot imagine letting some teenage boy take his innocent, little girl on a date because Daddy already knows how those boys think! Nope. He'd rather keep her at home — safe. Of course, unless you want your sweet baby to turn on you, Daddy, you'd better reconsider letting her out of the house!

Here's a thought. You want your daughter to know what she's getting herself into and how to protect herself from the wrong boys, right? Guess what! You have a teaching opportunity staring you in the face. Show her how it's done. *You* take her on a date, Dad. Pick her up at the door, "greet her parents" (improvise here!), open the car door, and take her to dinner. This is your chance to show your unknowingly naïve baby girl how a good guy treats ladies. If you teach her that she should be treated with respect, kindness, and boundaries, then she will learn to expect it. You can get your foot in the door to prepare her for life mixed with men. Carpe diem, daddies!!

If you don't show an interest in your beautiful baby girl, then someone else will, and you won't get to choose who that someone is. Influence her thought processes by being a great example of a loving guy in her life. Make her mind and heart yearn to date a man that her daddy would pick for her — someone a bit like Christ.

Something else I can tell you from experience is that if you don't take the time to help her grasp just how boys think — she won't know. She will listen to her friends and be utterly clueless. All the while, she'll

Ariel Allison and Shelby Rawson

believe she's got the opposite sex figured out fairly well. This usually means that she will be keenly aware of her body and the clothing that covers (or doesn't cover) it. She'll learn how to catch their eye — and she'll like it. For all she knows, the guys just think she's pretty and the attention feels good. You give her the right kind of attention first, and she'll know what to look for. Don't leave your daughter to her own devices in the dating world. Can I say it again? Prepare her!! Win her heart once more and prepare her.

This brings me to another issue. Time. You won't be able to do this without devoting time to her. You know what? That's perfect because she needs to know she is worth your time. Not your credit card or your $20 bill, but your time. Even if it's not hours and hours, just make the minutes focused on one thing — her. She needs to believe that her presence in your life matters. She needs to know that her heart and her zany ideas are not just peanuts to you. Don't tell her that her goofy ideas are stupid and brush them aside. Let her speak silliness to you and laugh with her . . . dream with her . . . and yes, cry with her. Her emotions are going to be all over the place — just like her thoughts and ideas. Listen and love her in your time together. Shoot baskets, eat ice cream, go for a walk, and shepherd your daughter's tender heart.

Your loving embrace is important now, more than ever. If you deprive her of that, she will seek it in the arms of other men. It can be incredibly awkward to see your little girl begin to develop breasts, curves, and hips. Your baby is becoming a woman right before your eyes, and you honestly don't know what to do about it. It probably makes you very uncomfortable. Keep one thing in mind — your daughter is not going to translate a hug from her father into something sexual, and if you begin to deprive her of affection she's always had, she will begin to wonder what is wrong. She may even begin to grow ashamed of the changes taking place in her body.

It is also during these years that your daughter is going to become aware of your faults. This usually doesn't happen until later in the teenage years, but it does happen. If you project an "I'm always right about everything" attitude you will create an emotional disconnect with her. She will be afraid to share her thoughts and feelings with you. She will feel as though it is not safe to reveal the inner workings of her heart. When she begins to feel that lack of safety with you, she will begin to hide things from you.

Daddy, Do You Love Me?

It can be exasperating to stay emotionally connected with a dingy teenager who only wants to talk about boys and clothes. The art to keeping the heart of your daughter during adolescence is looking for important life lessons in the seemingly insignificant conversations. So she wants to talk about boys — help her understand what kind of boy she should spend her time with. So she wants to talk about clothes — help her understand that the way she dresses affects the men around her. Ask lots of questions. What is she struggling with in school? What kind of movies is she watching? What kind of music is she listening to? Be available when she has questions for you. More than anything else, just listen. She wants to be heard, and she wants to know that her voice has value in your ears.

The Grown Daughter: College, Marriage, Kids

This stage in the father-daughter relationship can be especially difficult because you have been replaced by another man. You are no longer the most important man in her life. When your daughter marries, it can seem as though you either lose her completely, or she no longer needs you. Both of those are false. She may be another man's wife, but she will always be your little girl. She may be provided for and protected by another man, but no man can replace the role of father in her heart.

You can totally relate to the intro from the movie *Father of the Bride:*

I used to think a wedding was a simple affair. Boy and girl meet. They fall in love. He buys a ring. She buys a dress. They say, "I do." I was wrong. That's getting married. A wedding is an entirely different proposition. I know. I've just been through one. Not my own, my daughter's — Annie Banks-MacKenzie. That's her married name — MacKenzie. I'll be honest with you. When I bought this house years ago, it cost less than this blessed event . . . in which Annie Banks became Annie Banks-MacKenzie. I'm told that one day I'll look back on all this . . . with great affection and nostalgia. I hope so. You fathers will understand. You have a little girl . . . an adorable little girl who looks up to you . . . and adores you in a way you could never have imagined. I remember how her little hand used to fit inside mine . . . how she used to love to sit on my lap and lean her head against my chest. She said I was her hero. Then the day comes when she wants to get her ears pierced . . . and wants you to drop her off a block before the movie theatre. Next thing you know, she's wearing eye shadow and high heels. From that moment on you're in a constant state of panic. You worry about her going out with the wrong kind of guys . . . the kind of guys who only want one thing. And you know exactly what that one thing is . . . because it's the same thing you wanted when you were their age. Then she gets a little older . . . and you quit worrying about her meeting the wrong guy . . . and you worry about her meeting the right guy. And that's the biggest fear of all because . . . then you lose her. And before you know it, you're sitting all alone in a big, empty house . . . wearing rice on your tux, wondering what happened to your life.[2]

The warm daydreams you had are mixed unmercifully with the cruel reality that you never thought it would be this hard to raise a little girl. Then you wake up one day and she is grown with a family of her own, and you are no longer the most important man in her life. While you had that role for a while, it was short lived.

The fact is that your precious little girl is going to grow up one day and be someone's wife. Think of your own wife for a moment. Did her father instill a sense of self in her? Have you spent a lifetime rebuilding her self-esteem because her daddy tore it down? Was she even capable of receiving the love you tried to give her, or was her heart so confined that your relationship ended in disaster?

It is so important for you to help her learn to trust her husband in the area of finances. Do not throw money at her. It will only undermine her ability to trust her husband to provide for her. It can be a difficult transition for both of you, but one that is necessary for her well-being.

Hugs, kisses, and emotional encouragement are just as important as they ever were. She still needs to be hugged, to be told she is beautiful. Yet your affirmation during this season of her life needs to change. She needs to be affirmed by you as wife and mother. She needs to be encouraged and told she is doing a great job. She needs to know that her father approves of the choices she is making. She also needs that same shoulder to cry on when life gets hard and when tragedy strikes. You are every bit as important to her as you ever were. You role in her life is just one that changes every year. It will look different in each stage of her life.

Daddy, Do You Love Me?

There are some fathers reading this who have completely missed their daughter. You simply were not there for most of her life, or perhaps you were there but were completely uninvolved. Perhaps she is 40 years old and you think you don't stand a chance at winning her heart back. You couldn't be more wrong. I do think we women lose more of our courage to confront our wounded hearts the older we get, but I also know women who have gone to that dark place with their fathers later in life and they are reaping the rewards of a relationship denied them for half a century. It is never too late to do the right thing.

There is hope for the dad who has awakened to his failure when most would consider it "too late." While you are both still breathing, there is hope. Just like she had no control over your bad choices while she was growing up, neither do you have control over her rejection of you now. You cannot choose for her, but you can give her reasons to *choose* you. You must go back to the drawing board. You must acknowledge your mistakes. You must pursue her regardless of her response, and you must not give up. The only expectation she has for you is failure. There can be no quitting this time. She is worth the effort, far more than you will ever realize.

DIVORCED DADS

The reality for many, many of you fathers out there is the fact that you don't even live in the same house as your daughter. There is a separation between you, not only in your hearts, but physically as well. There has been a major rift between you and her mother and that relationship no longer exists. Or so you think. The fact is however, the relationship does exist because she is a product of it.

Dads, there is something I would beat you over the head with if I could. (Or, at least, several lashings with a wet noodle!) Your daughter should never suffer because of your relationship with your wife or ex-wife. Never. Your little girl is not to blame for the sins of her mother. Do not make her bear the burdens of your marriage. No matter how angry you are with her mom, it is between the two of you — not the three of you. Every time you make a choice influenced by your anger, rage, hurt, or malice toward your wife, your daughter feels it. Each time you spout off with a little dig on her mom, those words begin to stockpile in a little heart. One day, she will realize what you're doing and the results will be ugly. Do not be a stumbling block to your child. If your wife has done things that make you angry, there will be a day when your daughter will see her mother's mistakes all by herself. Allow her to make some realizations on her own.

Let's talk about finances. Yes, it is a good thing for a child to understand the ways of money as she grows. However, she doesn't need to know that her existence causes you financial strain. You may be thinking to yourself, "Well, I don't want her to think I can afford to give her everything." Good point. However, that's not *my* point. I am not encouraging you to give your daughter every indulgence and spoil her. I am encouraging you to protect your daughter from feeling like she is just another one of your financial obligations. If you write support checks every month, that should stay between you and your ex-wife. If extra expenses come up, that discussion should take place between you and her mother. Maybe when she gets older and has a job, the three of you can sit down and have a realistic, loving discussion about things that your daughter wants, but you may not necessarily be able to afford. When she is mature enough, you can help her understand the realities of money a little better. If you don't grasp this concept, you will more than likely wound your little girl. She will feel like a burden with a price tag attached to her forehead. And, when she marries, she will not know how to trust her husband in the area of money. Your little girl should not grow up believing she was an obligation to you. Instead of conveying to her that money is the treasure, show her that she is your treasure.

A PERFECT FATHER

I don't think there are many men that go into this "father" thing expecting to give up, or believing themselves capable of making terrible choices. No man wakes up one day and says to himself, "I am going to destroy my daughter." It begins with small choices that deaden the heart.

There are only two kinds of dads reading this book: those that have failed in their jobs with their daughters, and those who are trying to love their princesses well. Let me take a little pressure off right now, by saying that the only perfect Father is God. Every earthly dad is going to make mistakes and do things wrong. Perhaps a lot of things wrong. The question for you today, is how quickly do you run to make it right?

> But for you who fear My name, the sun of righteousness will rise with healing. . . . He will restore the hearts of the fathers to their children and the hearts of the children to their fathers (Mal. 4:2–6; NAS95).

Daddy, Do You Love Me?

God intended you to always, always, have access to the heart of your daughter. That relationship can be incredibly tender and enriching for both of you. It is so different than the one she has with her husband. She has to *learn* to love him. She came from the womb in love with you.

There are a million and one ways that a father can affect the heart of his little girl, but there is no other reality more important than the fact that your daughter's view of you will directly affect her view of God. We refer to God as Father. That word carries a great deal of significance. When you corrode the meaning of fatherhood in her heart, she will spend a lifetime struggling with trust. If you don't provide for your daughter, she will always wonder if God is going to come through for her. If you abandon her, abuse her, or neglect her, she will struggle deeply with her view of God's goodness.

It is really scary to be a parent. Believe me, I know. I have children. Sometimes I wonder if the best I can do for them is start saving today for the therapy they will need later! God does not expect you to be perfect. He knows better than that. He knows *you* better than that! What He expects from you is love and tenderness and effort. He expects you to try as hard as you possibly can to raise a daughter who knows she is loved, protected, and treasured. He expects you to apologize when you are wrong, but most importantly He expects you to depend on Him to learn how to raise that child.

When all is said and done, your daughter should have an accurate and beautiful portrait of God because of how you treated her, loved her, and cared for her. Your greatest calling as a father is to point her in the direction of her true Father. If you do that, you have done well.

Shelby's Thoughts

I will be painfully honest. Relationships with the opposite sex have never been one of my strengths. It's not that I couldn't manage to get one started. Nooo, it's definitely not that. It's more like I couldn't manage to stick to one. Excluding one guy my senior year of high school, every other guy I dated (until I met my husband) pretty much got a three. Three dates, that is. For one thing, I was too busy for a committed relationship when I was in school. That doesn't bother me. What does bother me to this day is how they all ended — in avoidance. When I thought I needed a change, I just started avoiding them LIKE THE PLAGUE! Needless to say, it pretty much never ended pretty.

Ariel Allison and Shelby Rawson

For years, I convinced myself that it was all about my lack of time and their being too clingy (or whatever excuse I could come up with). Now I know different. Now I know that the truth of the matter is that I was oblivious. I was completely oblivious as to how to relate to a guy I was dating in a healthy way. I had no boundaries or communication skills. I merely had walls — lots and lots of walls, and at that time, I wasn't aware that I was perched perfectly behind them. Sadly, there were some really nice guys who deserved better than the cold shoulder they received.

After my not-so-huge dating successes in high school and college, life in the real world was waiting for me. Single in the city. Wehoo. How exciting. At this point, I had time to reflect on the "tramplings" of my past and I felt fairly certain that marriage was going to be a hard row to hoe. As much as I had prayed that God would help me in this area, I continued to struggle.

Then I met Davy Rawson. Soon, my two-month dating record would be history. Davy was different. He was the first guy who appeared to want to get to know me. He wanted to know what made me tick. Wow. For the first time, I felt like someone wasn't just dating the homecoming queen or the cheerleader. Davy just wanted to date the girl who could throw the football.

Initially, the idea of being known was wonderful. It was what I had dreamed about for so long. Unbeknownst to me, something inside me was holding back. I was not aware of the fear that gripped me like an unfriendly zipper. (You know the kind. They seem to be friendly zippers and then . . . yyouch! You zip some skin.) The fear was just lying there. Hiding in the shadows and daring me to try to make a move.

So three rocky years later when I took his name, it came out of the shadows and slapped me. The fear that once kept a low profile decided to rear its ugly head and play a cruel joke on me. It waited until just the right time — marriage. My new husband would willingly initiate conversations with me only to meet my friends — the Wall Family.

I cannot begin to list all of the roadblocks that we hit. (It would take another book!) One of the most glaring examples was my reaction to finances. Yes, I know, it is very typical to argue over finances in marriage. Fine. I agree with that statement. However, my reaction to a simple budget discussion wasn't normal. It wasn't just the usual disagreement over "his wants, her wants." We would simply be attempting to go over the numbers and my countenance changed. My words became sharp or

Daddy, Do You Love Me?

non-existent. My body would go rigid. I could feel my chest tightening. Davy tried approaching me every which way, but loose. No luck. My response stayed the same. Each time I lashed out and crawled further within myself.

That is just the tip of the iceberg. I could write pages and pages on the many times I have kept my husband at arm's length. The very man I craved to know me emotionally was being reduced bit by bit to a dusty pile of failed attempts to reach his wife. I wanted our issues to be all his fault, but I knew that wasn't anywhere near the truth. My internal battles were creating more external battles than I could count.

I was attempting to tread my way out of quicksand. That is still where I sometimes find myself today. Treading fiercely to keep my head above the muck I have swum in for so long. It stinks. Frankly, I despise it. I cannot stand the fact that I struggle so much in my relationship with my husband. For a long time I haven't been able to put my finger on the heart of the problem. I think I'm finally beginning to understand a little more of what lies beneath the glassy surface.

I am painfully realizing that performing doesn't pay off in a relationship. It is even less effective when paired with perfectionism. In remembering my childhood, I'm not sure when the performance thing became such an issue for me. I can recall playing cards as an eight year old and I earnestly believed that winning was a must. I *had to win* that stupid game of "war." As a matter of fact, I tried cheating just so I wouldn't lose the card game. Something in my young mind told me that it was not acceptable for me to lose. If I lost at that game, then what did that make me? A loser. My identity was such a mystery to me that performing and perfectionism became the only way I could identify myself. So, if I didn't have those things, Shelby wasn't okay. Shelby needed to perform and be perfect to feel normal — to feel halfway decent about herself.

I realize now that I was trying frantically to feel important to my dad. I wanted him to notice me, so I began what a lot of little girls do — performing. Performing probably began to take over just about every aspect of my life by the time I reached adulthood. And you know, performers are doers. Perfectionist performers, on the other hand, are doers who only want to do it if they can do it perfectly and get your approval. A very ugly, destructive combination.

As performance began seeping into the various aspects of my life it would prove to be debilitating. Not only wasn't it okay for me to fail on tasks or performances, but it wasn't okay for me to be wrong about something, either. For me, wronging someone, or being wrong, is not acceptable. To be wrong, in my mind, means that I am a loser. A failure. A disappointment. Because of this, defensiveness jumps to the forefront and takes over. My defenses take over so quickly that I cannot see beyond them. I can't see straight.

As you can imagine, it often takes me a very long time to see when I am wrong. Thus, it shouldn't surprise you that apologizing takes longer yet. That brings us to my life as a wife today. God is graciously showing me that performance doesn't make for a great marriage. It doesn't fill a man's heart. It doesn't befriend him and confide in him. Performance leaves him standing alone. It gives no instructions on how to contact the performer. It is like a never-ending riddle. It's that voice mail that picks up but won't let you leave a message.

I want so badly to be a violin — to know that I'm a violin. Then, Davy could pick up a bow and attempt to bring a song from his wife's heart. He is putting forth superman-like efforts to follow the Master's Hand so he can learn how to make music with me, and it breaks my heart. It breaks my heart to know that he cannot play an instrument who has yet to learn her name.

So I weep and I pray for God to reveal my song to me. I pray that He would teach my heart a melody so pure and instinctual that one gentle touch from my husband's hands would make me sing.

A Word from Davy

I won't begin to pretend like I know all there is to know about how Shelby's relationship with her father has affected her. I am anxious and excited, however, because I see her Heavenly Father taking her to places and unraveling who she is and where she has come from — all for His glory and kingdom. I am anxious because the roads He takes her (us) on are often rocky and not so much fun to travel. I'm excited, because I know they lead to a sweet place of trust and intimacy — not only with each other, but with our Heavenly Father as well, the One who created us.

You see, Shelby and I are at the beginning of our own journey together. We are learning how to do life with the one God has given as a blessing and lifelong companion. So I would like to share some of our story and two simple thoughts . . . what I know and what I wonder.

Daddy, Do You Love Me?

Shelby and I met one day in a park after church. A group of us were playing football. I just remember two girls could throw the ball really well and she was the prettier of the two. So there you have it — a total babe who was athletic. What more could a guy ask for? What more could I want? Not so fast.

Later that evening, the group got together to watch a movie at someone's house, when in walks this total bombshell with no shoes on. I wasted no time. As I began to introduce myself to this footloose and fancy free hottie, I was a little embarrassed when she said, "Davy, I'm Shelby. We met earlier at the park." BUSTED. Shelby has naturally curly hair and she straightened it before coming over that evening (maybe because she thought I'd be there!). Okay . . . embarrassed, yes, but at the same time I thought — *I've hit the jackpot*. A total babe who was athletic *and* could look like two different girls by the way she wore her hair!! What more could a guy ask for? What more could I want? Not so fast.

Only minutes later, as I began to pursue and engage this beautiful creature, I noticed the first glimpse of Shelby's past. I'll never forget the looks on her face and her body language. They were as if to say, "You can't hurt me. I don't trust you. I'm interested in you, yes. I wonder what you're like, but keep your distance. Don't even think about hurting me." Painfully, much of our relationship today is still this way.

Shelby has had a hard time trusting me — the man in her life, her one, true companion, her husband. Well, yeah. Can you blame her?

It seems as though, for a little girl, a healthy picture of who she is, how a man of character should treat her, and how to recognize this kind of man should come from her dad — or at least a positive male figure. (Although, I wonder if girls always long for this figure to be their dad.) If Dad is not there to show her these things, she won't understand a good man and his ways, or how to trust him. We learn to trust people because they build trust first, show us they have good intentions, good character, and will not hurt or take advantage of us for their own benefit. Trust is earned, and I would venture to say that it is extremely difficult for a girl to even go there — to let a man earn her trust — if she hasn't had someone there to set a good example of what this trust looks like . . . Dad.

I hope and pray with all my heart that our daughter will know what kind of man she can trust, marry, and give herself to because of the example I have set by loving her and her mother well. I hope she will have seen how to seek God's kingdom and His righteousness first, how a man

Ariel Allison and Shelby Rawson

loves his wife, what a safe and secure home feels like, how to treat others with love and respect, how to forgive and ask forgiveness, how to be gentle and kind, tender and strong, serious and silly, honest and loyal, how to commit and follow through, how to be a good friend, and how to hope and dream. This I hope and pray.

Shelby and I are frequently working through her feeling/thinking that she is a disappointment to me, not a good enough wife or mommy and a failure. For example, sometimes I will give an opinion contrary to what she thinks or contrary to something she has already done, and she will *feel* or — as we learned in counseling — *think* those things. What we've learned she is actually *feeling* is one or more of a combination of eight core feelings (anger, hurt, sadness, loneliness, shame, guilt, fear, and gladness). These thoughts of being a disappointment, not being good enough and a failure are deeply rooted in her. They can disrupt her whole countenance and completely turn her 180 degrees. Often they will shut her down. Shelby grew up thinking she was a disappointment to her dad and that her sister was the favorite. No matter how hard she tried, she could not get her dad's praise, recognition, or approval. Whether she excelled at performing in show choir, achieving good grades, becoming Homecoming Queen, or just being "good," in her eyes, it wasn't good enough. She was failing with her dad. Dad's voice was not heard. So naturally I, being her spouse, bring all these same thoughts and feelings to the surface. It's almost as if they are programmed in her even though the circumstance may not fit the thought or feeling.

The funny, interesting, awful, beautiful, terrible, awesome, crummy, and kinda cool thing about spouses is that God made us the key that will inevitably unlock and open the luggage of one another's messy stuff. Without even trying to go there — it just happens. Shelby will often keep me at bay, avoid, not engage, and keep her distance because she knows I hold this key. Even as I write these words, I'm not someone she is able to trust or knows how to trust. Though she wants to, she's just not sure . . . it doesn't feel safe. Her past puts a stamp on it — approves it. Shelby was not taught to talk out her feelings — especially with a man. (I wonder if most of us were not taught this.) No father figure in her past proved to be trustworthy, constant, or committed. Though I understand Shelby somewhat, this distance often leaves me frustrated, alone, without a companion, longing for her intimacy, wanting to know her, and wanting to be known.

Daddy, Do You Love Me?

I'll never forget one evening I came home from work frustrated, feeling like a failure, a loser — the weight of the world had me down. After taking some of my frustration (undeservedly) out on Shelby, I went out and sat on the porch swing in the dark — alone. A few minutes later, Shelby came out, sat by my side, and handed me a picture frame with words written in it she'd previously given me as a gift. They read:

Provider — protector — precious
Lover — listener — leader
Strength — support — servant
Wise — willing — worthy
Courage — constant — comfort

She nailed it. The weight was gone. There was wind in my sail once again. Shelby somehow knew that I was — and could be — all these things in an awesome way with Christ's love and guidance. Maybe even more than that, I later realized that these things are what she longs for *me to be* in an awesome way. These are words that define a man. Words of trust. A man she can trust. I'll never view that frame the same way.

I can't help but wonder if a little girl's picture of Christ largely comes from her dad . . . and if that relationship is broken, then how does she view Christ?

When Shelby and I were dating, she made a phone call to her dad. (At this point, their relationship was severed.) He was not there, so she left him a message saying, "No matter what, I forgive you and I love you." Shelby is the most forgiving person I know. I've never seen anything like it. It blows me away. This is a gift God has given her. She has learned it from no one else. It gives me hope to know that no matter how much I mess up with my wife or children, that God — if He sees fit — can and will step in and fill their picture frame with words and gifts like forgiveness.

When I heard the news that Shelby's dad had called her back saying, "I love my little, curly-headed girl and I hope that you can forgive me," I began to see a change in Shelby. A change that is still growing and flourishing.

As I was writing, God put it on my heart to pause and observe (as I so often do) His beauty of the great outdoors. It is spring time, and the beautiful rolling hills of Tennessee are blooming with leaves and flowers. This is how I have seen Shelby change through the years. The leaves are

Ariel Allison and Shelby Rawson

filling in, the flowers are blooming. It is not complete. It is not finished. Yet it is beautiful and good.

As a dad, I have the most awesome opportunity to pass on to my daughter her own picture frame with words of Christ's love and revelation. Words that will help identify her in Christ — words that will give her courage, comfort, strength, and security. Words she will long to hear — words she will look for in a husband. I have the opportunity to show her love, recognition, and acceptance that will begin the flower's bloom in her own heart. Thankfully, I can rest knowing that God will complete the words, the change, the flower's bloom . . . just as He does in spring.

> *Dear God,*
>
> *Thank You for allowing me to be a dad to Kinsley and husband to Shelby. I have learned — and am learning — how to be a good dad and husband through our marriage and Shelby's past. I love them both dearly. Thank You for Your sovereignty. Amen.*

I have recently learned that when a man brings tenderness and strength together and interlocks them — just as our hands come together in prayer — he brings safety and security to those around him. A place of trust. I've found that I have a hard time putting the two together. I can be very strong at times, and I can be very tender, but to mesh them so that they form their own entity is a whole different thing for me. I praise God, however, because He has blessed me with the ability to bring tenderness and strength as I relate to our daughter — I thank God often for that gift. On the other hand, I especially have a hard time bringing the two together as I relate to Shelby. I don't know why just yet. It has become extremely evident to me that as dads and husbands, we must seek God's hand in providing tenderness and strength to our families. A place of safety, security, and trust. How huge this is for my wife — considering her past.

Shelby, I pray that you will be able to truly trust a man for the first time in your life because I have brought you tenderness and strength through Christ in me.

> Dear Shelby,
>
> I know you have always longed to feel special and important, and even though I once cringed out of my own insecurity at the thought of writing this small portion, God has used this as a sweet blessing. It is a constant reminder, with every slash and

Daddy, Do You Love Me?

swirl, every jot and tittle, every turn of my pen, every thought that is real, just how special and important you truly are.

I love you and am so proud of you for writing this book,

Davy

Ariel's Thoughts

It seems as though the analogy of music haunts my marriage. In particular, it is singing that has become a recurring theme. As you read earlier in this book, my ability and my desire to sing was utterly and unequivocally crushed at five years old. Only once in my life have I ventured to overcome that fear, and it ended in disaster, the most embarrassing moment of my life. I joined a Christmas choir one year, thinking that in a group my voice would be hidden, and I could learn to crawl from my shell. It turned out to be less "Caroling in the Park" and more "Brooklyn Tabernacle Choir." It was pretty horrible when I was asked not to sing in the accapella song. My pride wouldn't let me quit entirely, so I just lip-synched the other songs.

Several years later I found myself married and in counseling, trying to work through some of the issues I had with my dad. As we talked about my childhood, the story came up that I have told you. Shut down at five years old with a guitar. Interesting to note I never tried to learn guitar, either.

For some reason, that particular incident about my childhood stuck and we talked about it most of the session. The counselor asked if I had ever sung for my husband. I would have laughed at him had I not been crying. Of course not. That was far too risky. I already knew what happened when I sang for people.

I was horrified when he gave me my "homework." I was to go home and sing my favorite worship song, *Jesus I Am Resting, Resting*, to my husband. The words had not come from his mouth when the old familiar panic began to rise in my throat. I actually thought I would throw up on the spot.

For those who know me, it will come as no surprise that I am not capable of ignoring such challenges. I listened to that song every time I was in the car for two weeks. I played it over and over and over, practicing. Ashley knew I was going to sing it for him, and he would occasionally ask me about my plans.

I couldn't believe I was actually going to sing for Mr. "Steve Perry Sound-Alike Man," "Mr. he can sing any Journey song on the planet

Ariel Allison and Shelby Rawson

make it sound better than the original." You see, I am married to a real singer. Not a sing in the shower kinda guy. My husband can wail. He has phenomenal pipes, and little old "I can't carry a tune in a bucket me," was going to sing for *him*. Perhaps the horror of my situation sounds funny to you, but to me it was excruciating. I was about to bear one of my worst wounds.

Two weeks after my counseling appointment, I sang for my husband. I didn't have the courage to sing it on my own, so I sang along to the CD. I wasn't any good at all. My voice sounded horrible. I was scared and I was crying. But you know what? I wasn't crying as hard as my husband. Though it was not beautiful music I was making, not by any stretch of the imagination, my husband delighted in what he heard. When I became so overcome with emotion that I could no longer sing, he finished the song for me. His voice covered mine and made me sound *beautiful*.

I'm not going to say that I sing for my husband all the time now, because I don't, but we sing "Jesus Loves Me" to our boys when we put them down at night, and we sing it *together*. I know he hears all my mistakes, perhaps he even cringes on the inside, but I also know that he loves the fact that his wife is singing out loud. It is not pretty music that I am making, but he is letting me try, and he does not make me feel stupid for doing it wrong.

The analogy of music is one that my husband knows well. He is one of those freaks of nature that came from the womb knowing how to sing, and he sings better than most men I have ever heard, and then he gets a curve ball when he marries me, a woman terrified of making music. My poor husband is married to a woman afraid to sing.

Somehow Ashley has been given the grace to play this violin well. For the first time in my life I feel as though I am capable of making music. In his arms I feel as though just maybe I could sing — heck, there are times I feel I could *fly*.

Men are you hearing this? Are you feeling it? For those husbands and fathers and important men in our lives, do you see the power you hold over that girl? Power to do her good and not harm. Power to heal the most devastated places of her heart. Power to bring her freedom and hope. You are the bow that can bring forth the most beautiful music on earth. There is great redemption in your touch.

If you are a dad reading this and you have really screwed up, you need to know that you can heal the heart of your daughter. You can't erase the

Daddy, Do You Love Me?

past, but you can build a future that will set her heart free and will bring glory to God. If you are a husband and you have been playing your wife wrong for years, you can learn to play her songs, the songs that only she can sing. It is not too late to learn how to make music. As a good friend of mine says, "It is never too late to do the right thing."

The heart of the woman you love is learning how to rest in the goodness of God, learning who her true Father is.

> Jesus I am resting, resting,
> In the joy of what Thou art;
> I am finding out the greatness
> Of Thy loving heart.
> Thou hast bid me gaze upon Thee,
> And Thy beauty fills my soul,
> For by Thy transforming power,
> Thou hast made me whole.
> Jesus I am resting, resting, in the joy of what Thou art;
> I am finding out the greatness of Thy loving heart.
> Simply trusting Thee, Lord Jesus,
> I behold Thee as Thou art,
> And Thy love, so pure, so changeless,
> Satisfies my heart;
> Satisfies its deepest longings,
> Meets, supplies its every need,
> Compasseth me 'round with blessings:
> Thine is love indeed!
> Jesus I am resting, resting, in the joy of what Thou art;
> I am finding out the greatness of Thy loving heart.
> Ever lift Thy face upon me
> As I work and wait for Thee;
> Resting 'neath Thy smile, Lord Jesus,
> Earth's dark shadows flee.
> Brightness of my Father's glory,
> Sunshine of my Father's face,
> Keep me ever trusting, resting,
> Fill me with Thy grace.
> Jesus I am resting, resting, in the joy of what Thou art;
> I am finding out the greatness of Thy loving heart.[3]

Ariel Allison and Shelby Rawson

A Word from Ashley

How do I love my broken wife? Well, to be honest I don't know if I do a very good job, but I'm learning. Even after five years of marriage, I am still getting to know her. When we were dating, Ariel shared a lot with me about the lack of relationship between her and her dad. I could tell early on that her father had left a deep wound. What I didn't know was just how deep the wound really was. The damage done to her heart has affected our marriage a great deal.

Shortly after we were married, her father became ill and I began to see this beautiful little girl who so badly wanted to be loved by her dad. I was sad to see my wife so angry with him, yet desiring his love. Trust me, I'm a "fix it" kinda guy but I didn't have the tools to fix this. Nine times out of ten I didn't have a clue what to say when she shared something with me. So I learned to keep my mouth shut. When I heard all that stuff, I needed time to process. After thinking and praying, I could come back to her with rational answers, tender solutions, and encouragement. What happened when I didn't process, was probably what happens to most men: open mouth — insert foot — feel really bad for a long time.

To be honest, there were many days I wanted so badly to tell her "just drop it, and let it go," but I knew that saying something like that would have crushed her heart again, just like when she was five years old. It would have been the music thing all over again. I didn't want to be the second man in her life to crush her.

I am so proud of the way Ariel pursued her dad even until the day he went home. She never gave up on him saying, "I love you." I remember the day I came home from work and we sat down and she shared that her dad had finally told her that he loved her. It was the beginning of a long healing process that still continues today. I knew he loved her, he just didn't know how to express that love *to* her.

So how do I love this woman? I can't sit here and pretend that it comes naturally to me. I don't think it comes naturally to any man. I guess for me when I think of how to love, I have to go back to my best earthly example and that would be my dad. He did a really good job of modeling for me how to love your wife. I am very fortunate to have a dad that loves, cares, gives, and listens. . . . Did you hear that? He listens. I think that is a strength I get from my dad, listening and knowing that I can't fix everything. Sometimes the best thing is just to listen. I know

Daddy, Do You Love Me?

there have been many times Ariel has shared something deep with me and I sit there with the "deer in the headlights" look, totally inadequate to handle what she just unloaded on me.

She asked me recently if I felt like I didn't sign up for the baggage that she brought into our marriage, but the truth is, we all have baggage. I brought my own struggles and insecurities with me. The bottom line is that you don't go into a relationship thinking your spouse doesn't have issues. We were just lucky to know about each other's issues in advance. However, I think one of our strengths is that we talk and listen to each other in a rational way. It doesn't always happen like that, but for the most part we really try.

What Ariel really wants is just to be heard and loved. She doesn't want me to fix her. She knows that I *can't* fix her. I try to be slow to answer, because the fact is, she doesn't always need an answer. She just wants to know that I place value on her thoughts and opinions. She wants to know that her struggles matter to me. The truth is that we are all inadequate — the only one adequate to handle her pain is God himself. I cannot meet all of her emotional needs when she is wounded — some of that has to come from God alone. I can hold her, but I cannot heal her.

If I were to leave men with one thing to take away from this portion of the book, I would say be quick to hear what she is trying to communicate. Use a Q-tip every day and practice being a listener.

When Ariel "volunteered" me to write a small section of this chapter it kind of freaked me out. You see, just as she said earlier, I'm a music guy. It comes natural to me. I'm not a writer by any stretch. It's just not my gig. In fact, it's one of *my* biggest fears. So as I was reading this chapter, it smacked me upside the head that God brought two opposites together whose fears are the other's strength. Ariel and I are very different in a lot of ways, but we also complement each other really well, which I think is pretty cool. When you know your wife's strengths, it allows you to give her the freedom to pursue her passions, thus eliminating a lot of tension in your marriage. It also allows you to dream with her, while at the same time understanding the fears she wrestles with.

As I leave this start (and finish) to my writing career, I just want to say that my violin is battered and scarred, but the work that the Master *has* and *is* doing makes my violin a priceless treasure. I'm just a bow that's trying to move gently across the strings, trying to make some music for the Kingdom.

Ariel Allison and Shelby Rawson

Ariel, I love you. You are more beautiful than the day we met. You are more than I deserve in a wife. You are a fantastic mom to London and Parker, and I am truly enjoying making music with you.

Thank you for always looking to the Kingdom and challenging me.

Ashley

Endnotes

1. John Eldridge, *Wild At Heart: Discovering the Secret of a Man's Soul* (Nashville, TN: Thomas Nelson, 2001), p. 182.

2. *Father of the Bride* (Warner, 1991).

3. Words by Jean S. Pigott; music by David Hampton, ©1998, New Spring Publishing, Inc. CCLI, License No. 34305.

Daddy, Do You Love Me?

So What?

Past the seeker as he prayed came
the crippled and the beggar and the
beaten. And seeing them . . . he cried,
"Great God, how is it that a loving creator
can see such things and yet do nothing about
them?" . . . God said, "I did do something. I made you."
— Sufi teaching

Chapter
10

Your heart is free. Have the courage to follow it.
— William Wallace's father
Braveheart

"Would you tell me, please, which way I ought to go from here?"
"That's depends a good deal on where you want to get to."
— Lewis Carroll
Alice in Wonderland

*D*espite the dismal rain pouring outside, her heart felt lighter than it had in months. She would be the first to admit that she was afraid, but she felt more than that: anticipation, even hope. Her pen hovered over the paper as she stared out the window, watching rivulets of water run down the windowpane, and searching for the words to say.

She hadn't spoken to her father in five years, not since he left her mother her senior year in high school. He had married his secretary the day after the divorce was final. His efforts toward his daughter had been minimal, and her responses had been even less. She had made it perfectly clear that she never wanted to speak to him again, but that was five years ago. It had been a long five years, and she'd grown quite a bit, both as a woman and as a daughter.

She closed her eyes, took a deep breath, and the pen met paper.

Dear Daddy,

That was all she could write for 15 minutes.

A whirlwind of emotions raged inside her heart, paralyzing her hand. There was so much she wanted to tell him . . . about how badly he'd hurt her . . . about how her mother had cried herself to sleep every night for two years . . . about the hate and the anger and the shame that she felt. But none of those thoughts made it to the page. She wasn't pretending they didn't exist, but that was not the purpose of this letter.

Again her pen began to dance across the blank page.

I miss you. There, I said it. For five years I have been pretending that I don't miss you. I don't want to miss you, but the fact is that I have. I missed you at my high school graduation. I missed you the day I went off to college. I have missed you every Thanksgiving, Christmas, birthday (mine and yours), and all the days that have fallen in between. When you walked out the door, a piece of my heart left with you, and I have not been whole since.

We have so much to talk about, but this letter is not where I want that discussion to take place. I want to see you, Dad. I want to look in your eyes. I want to see if there is any more gray in your hair. I want to know if you miss me. I want to know how you are doing, what you are feeling, and what life has brought to you in the last five years. I want one of those giant bear hugs you used to give me when I was a little girl. More than anything, I want to start over. I know that life cannot be like it was. There is no going back. But we can begin again, and I want that more than anything.

I love you, Daddy. I always have.

Daddy, Do You Love Me?

It was then that she began to weep, a hard, sobbing cry that lasted for hours. The tide had risen in her heart and all the junk she'd swept out to sea resurfaced. She cried herself to sleep, and did not finish her letter that day. Or the next. Three weeks later she signed her name and sealed the envelope with a prayer. A month after that she finally found the courage to drop it in the mailbox. As it fell from her hands, she felt a load lift from her soul, and she knew she'd done the right thing.

She had done everything she could. What happened next was not up to her, nor should it be. She awaited the next chapter in a story written by divine hands.

WHERE DO WE GO FROM HERE?

In a few moments you will have finished another book. You'll set it on the night table or on the shelf. I don't know how long it took you to finish it, but I'm sure that you had a lot to digest, and I'm also sure that a lot of it was less than palatable, but it's almost over now. I hope you liked it. I hope it was life changing.

If you just lay it aside and say, "Oh yeah, I read that book," you are doing yourself a great disservice. It wasn't light reading material that you just went through.

So what? You're done with the book, what now? What are you going to do about everything you just read? Move on with your life? Complain that the authors don't know what it's like to be you? Shrug off all that stuff about forgiveness and honor? Excuse yourself from what God commands you to do?

If that is your choice, I can't stop you. As a matter of fact, I will never even know, but if that is what you do, you just wasted a lot of precious time, both mine and yours.

This book wasn't designed to be an expository to all the things that can go wrong in the father-daughter relationship. It was designed to be a tool that helps you take the next step. So take it. Just put one foot in front of the next. Take a leap full of faith and hope.

You have a lot of places you can go from here.

You can admit that your dad really let you down.

You can mourn what he did not give you.

You can begin to unravel your life from the bondage of abuse.

You can begin to approach God as your ultimate Father.

You can start the process of learning your dad's story.

Ariel Allison and Shelby Rawson

You can forgive your father. Or if you can't go there just yet, you can be willing to be *willing* to forgive your father.

You can write a tribute to your dad and honor him for the things that he did right.

You can begin the process of trying to find restoration with your dad and with your Heavenly Father.

You can assess how your relationship with your dad is affecting your marriage, or your relationship with other men in your life.

And there are many, many more options. I just covered a few. Regardless of what that first step is, or what order you take, you are giving yourself freedom and hope. You are receiving life.

THERAPY, COUSELING, AND ADVICE

One of the biggest steps for some of you may be walking through the door of a good counselor. You may need to go for no other reason than having a completely objective sounding board. It is very important to have someone who can listen to you spill your guts and pour out your heart without any pre-conceived notions. In addition, it is critical that this counselor points you in a healthy direction toward real healing. Real healing requires the help of the ultimate Counselor. Your guidance should be rooted in the love of God. It doesn't mean that all of your conversations should revolve around a campfire singing "Kumbayah." What it should mean is that your counseling sessions will be grounded to a secure faith in God. It means that you won't be talking to another person who thinks it's perfectly fine to hate your father for the rest of your life. You should walk out of his or her office being able to see a little bit of light at the end of your tunnel.

I realize you may be completely skeptical of this idea. I know that I was given the impression on more than one occasion that seeing someone for "therapy" was "okay for some people." There are a lot of people in this world who will be quick to tell you that counseling does not work, that all they do is mess with your head and give you thoughts that weren't real to begin with. I'm guessing that these are the same people who have no desire to work through their own issues. They would probably rather just "get over it." I've heard it before. And you know what? I didn't want to just get over it. I wanted to get through it, grow through it, learn from it, move beyond it, and finally feel healed. That's what I want for you. No sweeping it under the rug. There's already too much stuff hiding there. It's not time for hiding. It's time for healing.

Daddy, Do You Love Me?

There is absolutely nothing wrong with seeking help. It's not weak. It takes courage to admit you need help, open the door of a hurting heart, and pull back the scab of an all-too-painful wound that you'd rather forget. People in this world would have you believe that you don't need to do it. Satan would love to keep you at home, locked inside his lies. That cunning serpent would prefer it if your heart was never restored. He'd sooner keep his claws locked firmly around your throat than see you take steps toward rebuilding yourself. Do not let him win. If you need counsel, *then go for it.* This is your life. Your heart. Your future. Make the choice to take charge of it.

Personally, I've been to several counselors at different times in my life — and I will probably be going back again! Not because I'm a lunatic, but because I am still just a woman trying to cope in a world of chaos. Some of the time, counseling comes in the form of a mentor or a woman who is full of wisdom and His Word. It doesn't always take place in an office. There are many times when it happens on the sidewalk, a coffee shop, or on the phone (while my toddler chatters in the background). It doesn't matter where it happens, but it does matter who it is with. The point is this. There are all sorts of counselors to be had, but the important thing is choosing the ones who answer to their Holy Counselor.

FURTHER UP AND FURTHER IN

God does not want us to dwell in this place forever. It is okay to come here and examine our hearts, to lick our wounds, and to grieve, but it is not okay to stay here. Where then do we go? And how do we get there? I believe the heart of God is calling us further up and further in.

My guess is that you are sitting there today with fewer blinders on your eyes. The tears you have shed have washed them away and now you see your life, and the life of your father, in a whole new light. Sight is a beautiful thing. You view your life and the journey set before you. I am also hoping that you see something you have never seen before, a loving Father.

That Father is calling you to himself. "Come my daughter, and see how I can love you."

Further up into in His arms and further up into His love. There is room for you.

A scene from C.S. Lewis's *The Last Battle* describes the next leg of our journey perfectly:

"Come further in! Come further up!" [Aslan] shouted over his shoulder.

It was the Unicorn who summed up what everyone was feeling. . . . "I have come home at last! This is my real country! I belong here. This is the land I have been looking for all my life, though I never knew it till now." . . . "Don't stop," cried Farsight the eagle, "Further up and further in. Take it in your stride. . . ."[1]

That is what we feel about our lives and our hearts when God takes the broken, the abandoned, and the abused and redeems them into beauty. We recognize the old, and we remember it as well, but we are new creations and we now see our lives in the glory of what they were always meant to be. Our Daddy calls us further up and further in to His very own heart. He calls us to crawl on His lap and delight in the adoration and closeness of a tender Father captivated with the beauty and charm of His daughter.

Do you believe that the God of heaven wants to take your pain and your brokenness and use it for your good and His glory? Do you think that perhaps you have walked this road so that you might reach back to someone else and help them navigate the path? Do you think there is purpose in your pain? I do. That is why you hold this book in your hands.

Torch the fort! Learn how to love without impenetrable walls. Let somebody into your world. Don't make them suffer for the pain of your past. Love them with a heart that has been tendered by brokenness. Love them with a security that has been found through surrender.

Give better than you got. Don't choose to give love in the same doses it was seemingly received. Know your boundaries and extend grace to an imperfect man. Your past is just that — the past. Do not let it hold you prisoner in the present. You deserve a deeper life!

A Time for Everything in a Wounded Little Girl
An adaptation of Ecclesiastes 3:1–8 & 11

There is a time for everything, and a season for every purpose
under heaven:
A time to be born, and a time to die;
A time when you curse your birth and pray for death;

Daddy, Do You Love Me?

A time to plant and a time to uproot;

A time when the planted devastation must be displaced;

A time to kill and a time to heal.

A time he took life from the little girl who now must be restored;

A time to tear down and a time to build;

A time to look at the wreckage and piece together a new life;

A time to weep and a time to laugh;

A time to shed bitter tears and a time to rejoice in the life yet to live;

A time to mourn and a time to dance;

A time to grieve for a broken child and a time to sway to the rhythm of renewal;

A time to cast away stones and a time to gather stones together;

A time to tear down your walls and a time to guard your heart from destruction;

A time to embrace and a time to refrain;

A time to reach out in love and a time to hold back;

A time to search and a time to give up;

A time to seek answers to questions in your soul and a time to rest in not knowing;

A time to keep and a time to throw away;

A time to cling to the good and let go of the bad;

A time to tear and a time to mend;

A time to be a broken little girl and a time to be a healed daughter;

A time to be silent and a time to speak;

A time when your words must cease and your heart finds its voice;

A time to love and a time to hate;

A time to embrace fond memories and despise wretched remembrances;

A time for war and a time for peace;

A time to battle the demons raging within and to learn to rest in the shadow of your Daddy's wings;

For He has made everything beautiful in its time.

You will learn of your beauty.

Ariel Allison and Shelby Rawson

SO WHAT?

Or maybe I should say, "Now what? Where in the name of Cletus do I go from here?" Good question. I don't want to leave you hanging out there, just floundering in the breeze. This is the place in your life where the rubber meets the road. It's time to ponder all that you've read, make certain the millstone is off your neck, see to it that bitterness is no longer the bridle of your heart and move. Yes, move. Take some action so you can chuck out the chains you've been carrying and learn to finally let go.

I wish I could tell you exactly what you need to do; that there was an exact science to this whole step-taking thing, but I can't. I didn't write your story. I don't know your story. Your path belongs to you. When you make the choice to step forward, there is only one hand to hold. There is only one hand to keep you steady. Reach for the strong hand of the Father. Grab on to your Daddy's hand. He will stay beside you whether you leap, limp, run, walk, stagger, or crawl, and He won't leave you.

It is time for you to make a choice for your life. Do you want to live limping through each day with your heart stuck in an emotional cast? Or do you want to be free to experience all the highs and lows of living without shackles? (Yes, I still included the lows because that will be reality for all of us!) If you don't make a choice for the better, then logical consequences will take over. It won't get better. You will have learned to grieve and groan for your pain and misery, but missed the point — growth!

Growing is not always quick and easy. That is how a weed grows. It takes no time to develop good, strong roots. Who wants their life to look like a weed? Be a flower. Be an oak. Be an amazing garden. Take your time to make choices that will not wither at the first rattling wind. Pruning and weeding are required, of course. This would be where (yep, you guessed it) a little more pain may come into play. As you grow, you will notice some stray stems or branches that don't belong any more. Weeds, like lies, guilt, and discouragement will do their best to thrive around you and choke the new life right out.

Keep your eyes on the prize. Your heart needs to be the beautiful garden that the Master intends it to be. Beautiful gardens don't take shape and bloom overnight. There will be frustration and backsliding. You will think you've overcome something and it will creep back up on you forcing you to deal with it once more. You will have to fight against

Daddy, Do You Love Me?

the old "tapes" playing in your head telling you every negative thing about your life. Those "tapes" are worse than a little crabgrass in your garden. They are more like kudzu. Eventually, if let go, they will cover up all the beauty and make sure their presence is the only evident thing in your mind's eye.

Please, please don't be discouraged if reconciliation with your dad cannot happen. Sometimes, we have no choice in that matter. Sometimes, they give you no choice. I hate that. It grieves my heart. I want your story to have a happy ending. My hope is that you understand by now that there is a Dad who wants to be reconciled with you. God wants to have a relationship with His little girl. Yes, the same God that you may not be too crazy about wants you to be assured that He is your Daddy. He already knows that running with reckless abandon to Him may not happen. Your Father knows that His daughter may just take a hesitant, little step. He understands that you may still feel so wounded and tired that your strength to move is gone. That's okay, because God has been waiting with bated breath for His little girl to call out to Him. The King of heaven is waiting for His princess to make the slightest whisper in His direction so He can come running. He will meet you where you are — running, crawling, or stuck.

Honestly, I don't know what this point in the road looks like for you. I do know that it isn't the end. Different paths lie in front of you waiting to be traveled. Some of the roads will be easier than others. Learning to let go and forgive may take you on a longer road than you had hoped. The point is that you make a choice to step forward and walk down that path. The first step probably won't have a sudden, miraculous healing, but if you keep walking you will be walking toward healing. It would be naïve and shortsighted of me to let you believe that healing happens all at once. It happens in waves. The more you grow, the more you will heal.

If you do experience reconciliation with your dad, that is wonderful. It's more than wonderful, it's extraordinary. I pray that you will be patient with the shaky ground you may now be treading. Bear in mind, you are re-learning how to relate to someone you have probably known your entire life. It's probable that your relationship will feel like dancing with a partner for the very first time. Neither one of you may be too sure which way to move. Toes may be stepped on a few times. You may get annoyed with each other. You may even want to quit, but don't. You

Ariel Allison and Shelby Rawson

have waited a long time to dance with your dad. Give him a chance to learn some new steps.

Try to remember that dancing requires grace. We both know you have had a healthy dose of the realities of grace! Carry it with you if your dad attempts to move toward you. Chances are that he doesn't have a clue how you are wanting him to dance just yet, but he is trying, right? Maybe for the first time, your dad is making efforts to learn how to have a relationship with you. He may want the dance to end the same way you do — in an embrace.

WHAT IT LOOKS LIKE FOR US

The moment you picked up this book you saw that it was written by two different women. As you have read our "thoughts" at the end of each section, you saw that we have been polar opposites in how we have dealt with this wound, and also how this wound has dealt with us. We did that on purpose, to illustrate the fact that this journey looks different to every woman. There is no formula. There is no blueprint.

Both of us had a day where we *chose*. We chose to move forward. We chose to do something about our pain. Neither of us would have imagined that many, many years later we would have written a book, sharing the most fragile parts of our lives. We would have never imagined that our pain could be put to such good use. Never.

Neither of us will ever forget the day we decided to write this book. We were in the swimming pool on a very hot July day. We discussed why Ariel's father couldn't say he loved her, and we discussed why Shelby had always felt that God wanted to use her to encourage other women in this area, and we thought, *why not?* We aren't famous. We aren't models or actors. We are just stay-at-home moms trying to make the best out of life. Neither of us have been to seminary and one of us hasn't even been to college. We aren't *Bible* experts or theologians. We are just like you, normal women living day to day by the grace of God, and that is why we are qualified to write this book. We have *lived* it.

It is because we are so very normal that this book speaks so loudly. We weren't given any special help as we sifted through the damage done to our hearts. Both of us have been to counselors, but they weren't famous either. As a matter of fact, they were men and women who worked for local churches or were associated with them. There was nothing magic about our recovery. We weren't given roadmaps to healing, we were handed a

Daddy, Do You Love Me?

compass and pointed in the direction of the Healer. It is that same compass that we are passing on to you in this book. The hope we feel, we gladly share. The healing we have experienced, we encourage you to find, and dear friends, we will be with you each step of the way.

Ariel's Thoughts

My father has impacted the story of my life to a great degree. He is woven through my experiences, my beliefs about myself and God, and my DNA. He has played an integral part in everything that I am. Sometimes the role he played was unfortunate, but there were times that it was uplifting and holy. Tragic and triumphant. Lonely and lovely. This woman named Ariel is a walking contradiction of bruises and beauty. A pillar of grace that often feels like a pillar of salt. I am a living, breathing testimony to the fact that God makes "all things new" (Rev. 21:5).

I am almost 30 years into my journey and as I stop and survey my progress I almost want to weep. Because you see, I know that my Redeemer lives. Despite my humble beginnings, and my shattered heart, I am a new woman in Christ. Even more than that, the little girl in my heart is learning to sing for the first time. I am loved, and my voice is lovely to my Father. He longs for me to sing.

The "so what" to my journey is the fact that I can declare confidently that I have a daddy. I lost my father far too early, but that does not mean I am fatherless. The road that God has laid before me is one that leads to Him. My lessons and my struggles serve the purpose of teaching my heart who my true Father is. He wants me to trust Him. He wants me to depend on Him. He wants to delight in me. He wants me to let Him, and I often struggle because I don't know how.

All of the things that I am learning, and all of the ways that I am grow-ing cannot be shared with James Lee Allison. Because my earthly father is gone, I have been forced to run to my Heavenly Father. I will admit that it is awkward. I can't see Him and I can't touch Him. His embrace is not physical, but spiritual. I have nothing tangible because my journey is one of faith. I must have faith that my Father will provide for me, I must have faith that my Father will teach me how to be a daughter, I must have faith that my Father is good. Those are the core struggles of my heart, doubts that have very deep roots. Those are the honest yearnings of my soul and it is my Heavenly Father who desires to answer them.

Ariel Allison and Shelby Rawson

For every woman out there whose father has died, or who will never see restoration in this life, know that I am walking this road as well.

Don't walk alone. Take this journey with a friend. There were two people in my life who carried my heart the year my father died. The first was my husband who held me every night while I cried, and the second was my co-author and precious friend Shelby. She wrote the following poem for me that year. (It sits framed on my nightstand to this day as a reminder of the power of friendship.) She thought she wrote it to me as a thank-you for friendship, but in reality it is a testament to her and the friend she has been to me.

> For couch confiding,
> Wounded hearts shared,
> Walks of wisdom,
> And porch swing prayers. . . .
> For lingering laughter
> Followed by fears,
> Humbling happenings,
> And childhood tears. . . .
> For a woman of God,
> A noble wife,
> I thank You, Lord,
> For this friend in my life.

I am thankful for your courage in picking up a book like this and reading it all the way through. I am thankful that you have taken the time to listen to our hearts and to hear our stories. I am thankful that your story is unfolding before you, and I am thankful that this book has played a part in it. I am thankful for the quiet longing in your heart to have a Father. I am thankful that your longing will not go unmet. You have a Father who loves you desperately.

Shelby's Thoughts

At the end of our journey together, this is what I want you to know about me and where I am today. I am still struggling. Yes, my relationship with my dad turned around 180 degrees. Our relationship is not strained or stressed these days. But me? Just me? I struggle. I wiggle. I sometimes crawl in my relationships — particularly my marriage.

Daddy, Do You Love Me?

I am restored and reconciled both to my dad and my God. Yet, I am not done. I have taken the steps to work on a broken relationship, but that doesn't mean all of my baggage disappeared with the bitterness. No, as a matter of fact, my baggage is still being unpacked and separated. For the most part, I know what's in the suitcase, but every once in a while I'm unpleasantly surprised by something I thought had been sorted out!

So, basically, I am a work in progress. That alone frustrates me to no end some days. If you knew me personally, this would come as no surprise. Even my close friends know that I am still somewhat guarded. My husband certainly knows my tendency to put up walls without batting an eye — like a knee-jerk reaction. Half the time, I don't realize I'm doing it! I flounder in my insecurity and self-esteem. Quite often I get a little anxious when walking into a room full of people that I know . . . caught up in worrying if they will approve of me today. I don't know if I will ever believe that my legs are halfway attractive. So, as I sit here today, I am still a walking work in progress.

What I *can* tell you is that I am able to see patterns and behaviors more easily than in the past. Recognition is power. Once you can recognize when you are doing something that is a result of past wounds, it is much easier to change or stop the behavior. Obviously, for me, the change is taking time in some areas! This can be a source of irritation for me and my husband, as well. Unfortunately, he still bears the brunt of my not-always-speedy metamorphosis. As quickly as I want to be able to change from the critical caterpillar to a beautiful butterfly, it doesn't seem to work out that way in many instances.

One of the encouraging things that I've found in the midst of my metamorphosis is the knowledge of one fact. God is not finished with me yet. He's not turning His back on me in disgust as He watches me struggling to sprout wings. He is helping me to grow and change inside of this cocoon so I can break free and dance in the air of the unknown, instead of being caged inside of my fears. No, my Daddy isn't done teaching me, yet. I am learning more and more that His "perfect love casts out all fear" (1 John 4:18). Instead of clutching onto my cocoon for dear life, I'm finding that there is beauty in this butterfly. He gave it to me. God created my heart to be filled with splendor and loveliness — not scars and loneliness. My God — my Daddy — wants me to spread my wings, drink in the nectar of life, and fly.

Ariel Allison and Shelby Rawson

In my final thoughts, I wonder if you are like me. Struggling. Wrestling. Tapping at the cocoon around you, yet somehow afraid to break free and put yourself out there. Yes, out there, where you could possibly find hurt and humiliation, rejection and rage. Yet also out there where freedom waits for you, burdens are behind you, and your wings are no longer in want of the wind. Do you believe you are meant to drink in the sweet nectar of life instead of drowning in the dregs of darkness and despair? *You are.* Your wings are meant to be free to fly — not to stay forever bound tightly next to your heart. You are meant to risk again. You are meant to dance — not alone — but in the arms of a King.

My prayer is that if you learn to trust only one man, it is *the Man.* May He walk with you, hold you, and embrace you in your passage from pain to peace. May He shelter you in the storms of struggle, listen to your shouts of anger and cries of pain, answer your pleas for help and meet you in the dungeons of your desolation. May you never, ever feel truly alone or unloved again.

So, we leave you with one last thought: your Redeemer lives.

Who taught the sun where to stand in the morning?
Who told the ocean, you can only come this far?
Who showed the moon where to hide 'til evening?
Whose words alone can catch a falling star?

Well I know my Redeemer lives.
I know my Redeemer lives.
All of creation testifies
This life within me cries
I know my Redeemer lives.

The very same God that spins things in orbit
Runs to the weary, the worn, and the weak.
And the same gentle hands that hold me when I'm broken
They conquered death to bring me victory.

Now I know my Redeemer lives
I know my Redemer lives.
Let all creation testify
Let this life wihtin me cry
I know my Redeemer, He lives.

Daddy, Do You Love Me?

To take away my shame
And He lives forever I'll proclaim,
That the payment for my sin
Was the precious life He gave,
But now He's alive
And there's an empty grave.

And I know my Redeemer, He lives,
I know my Redeemer lives.
Let all creation testify,
This life within me cries
I know my Redeemer lives.

> "Redeemer," by Nicole C. Mullen,
> from the album *Nicole C. Mullen*

Endnote

1. C.S. Lewis, *The Last Battle* (New York: HarperCollins, 1994).

Counseling Resources

American Association of Christian Counselors
http://www.aacc.net/
Website includes: counselor locator, treatment centers, conferences

Christian Counseling and Educational Foundation
http://ccef.org/home.htm
Website includes: instructions on choosing a counselor, recommended reading material

The Minirth Clinic
http://www.minirthclinic.com
Website includes: counseling services, recommended reading material

Cloud-Townsend Resources
http://www.cloudtownsend.com
Website includes: curriculum, recommended reading material

Southern California residents: Please call our office for a list of counselors near you. 1-800-676-HOPE (4673) or 714/979-7590

Meier Clinics
http://meierclinics.org
1-888-7CLINICS (725-4642)
Website includes: counseling services, list of clinic locations

Focus on the Family
http://www.family.org
1-800-232-4673
Website includes: recommended reading material

Recommended Reading

FATHER/DAUGHTER ISSUES:
Longing For Daddy:Healing from the Pain of an Absent or Emotionally Distant Father by Monique Robinson (Colorado Springs, CO: WaterBrook Press, 2004).

Daddy, Do You Love Me?

Always Daddy's Girl: Understanding Your Father's Impact on Who You Are by H. Norman Wright (Ventura, CA: Regal Books, 1989).

You Are Your Father's Daughter by Dr. Earl R. Henslin (Nashville, TN: T. Nelson Pub., 1994).

Fatherneed: Why Father Care Is as Essential as Mother Care for Your Child by Kyle Pruett (New York: Free Press, 2000).

Tribute: What Every Parent Longs to Hear by Dennis Rainey with David Boehi (Nashville, TN: T. Nelson, 1994).

Wild At Heart: Discovering the Secret of a Man's Soul by John Eldridge (Nashville, TN: Thomas Nelson, 2001).

Captivating: Unveiling the Mystery of a Woman's Soul by John and Stasi Eldridge (Nashville, TN: Nelson Books, 2005).

SEXUAL ABUSE:
The Wounded Heart by Dan Allender (Colorado Springs, CO: NavPress, 1990).

Redeeming Love (Fiction) by Francine Rivers (Sisters, OR: Multnomah, 1997).

FORGIVENESS:
In the Grip of Grace by Max Lucado (Dallas, TX: Word Pub., 1996).

Forgive and Love Again by John Nieder and Thomas M. Thompson (Eugene, OR: Harvest House Publishers, 1991).

Forgive and Forget: Healing the Hurts We Don't Deserve by Lewis Smedes (San Francisco, CA: Harper & Row, 1984).

Art of Forgiving: When You Need to Forgive and Don't Know How by Lewis Smedes (Nashville, TN: Moorings, 1996).

VERBAL ABUSE
Tired of Trying to Measure Up by Jeff VanVonderen (Minneapolis, MN: Bethany House, 1989).

SPIRITUAL ABUSE
Churches that Abuse by Ron Enroth (Grand Rapids, MI: Zondervan, 1992).

The Emotionally Healthy Church by Peter Scazzero (Grand Rapids, MI: Zondervan, 2003).

Ariel Allison and Shelly Rawson

The Subtle Power of Spiritual Abuse by David Johnson and Jeff Van Vonderen (Minneapolis, MN: Bethany House Publishers, 2005).

SELF-ESTEEM ISSUES

Abba's Child: The Cry of the Heart for Intimate Belonging by Brennan Manning (Colorado Springs, CO: NavPress, 2002).

Codependent No More – Melody Beattie (New York: MJF Books, 1997).

BOUNDARIES

Boundaries by Henry Cloud and John Townsend, www.cloudtownsend.com.

CHOOSING A MATE

Avoiding Mr. Wrong (and What to Do If You Didn't) by Stephen Arterburn and Dr. Meg Rinck (Nashville, TN: Thomas Nelson Publishers, 2000).

Falling In Love for All the Right Reasons by Dr. Neil Clark Warren (New York: Center Street, 2005).

Finding the Love of Your Life by Dr. Neil Clark Warren (Colorado Springs, CO: Focus on the Family, 1992).

How to Get A Date Worth Keeping by Dr. Henry Cloud (Grand Rapids, MI: Zondervan, 2005).

TRUST ISSUES

Bold Love by Dan Allender and Tremper Longman III (Colorado Springs, CO: NavPress, 1992).

PORNOGRAPHIC ADDICTION

www.xxxchurch.com

"XXXchurch exists to bring awareness, openness, accountability, and recovery to the church, society, and individuals in the issues of pornography and to begin to provide solutions through non-judgmental and creative means."

SIN ISSUES

The Bondage Breaker by Neil T. Anderson (Eugene, OR: Harvest House, 2000).

Daddy, Do You Love Me?